THE
GLORY DAYS

THE
GLORY DAYS

Great West Indian Cricketers **25**

TONY KING & PETER LAURIE
FOREWORD BY SIR GARFIELD SOBERS

MACMILLAN
CARIBBEAN

Macmillan Education
Between Towns Road, Oxford, OX4 3PP
A division of Macmillan Publishers Limited
Companies and representatives throughout the world

www.macmillan-caribbean.com

ISBN 1 4050 1270 6

First published 2004

Printed in Thailand

Design by Ikon Design 246-434-4566

2008 2007 2006 2005 2004
10 9 8 7 6 5 4 3 2 1

CONTENTS

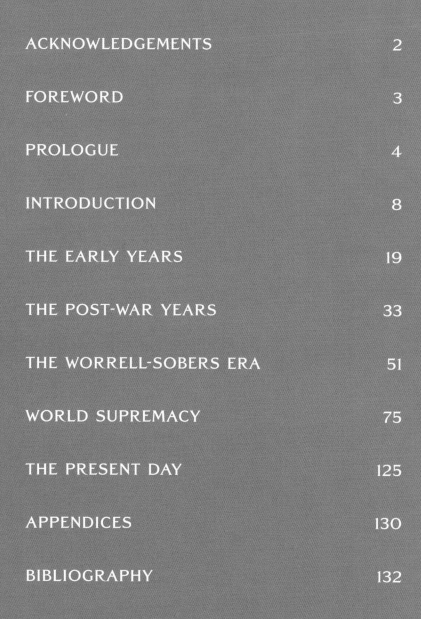

ACKNOWLEDGEMENTS

We had a great deal of help putting this book together. We want to thank James Gardiner for suggesting it in the first place, and Gordon Brooks for some of the superb photographs.

Special thanks to Sean Field and Alison Forde Alleyne of Ikon Design for the brilliant design.

We deeply appreciate The Right Excellent Sir Garfield Sobers graciously agreeing to write a foreword to the book. Many others offered helpful suggestions and criticisms, not least in the choice of the twenty-five.

There are too many persons to thank, but even at the risk of leaving out some we have to mention: Tony Cozier, Wilmot Bourne, Anton Dick, Caroline Gardiner, Jason King, Michael King, Sterling Mungal, Peter Roberts and Mrs. H. Sealy.

FOREWORD

BY THE RIGHT EXCELLENT SIR GARFIELD SOBERS

It is a pleasure to write the foreword to THE GLORY DAYS, a timely reminder of the great tradition of West Indies cricket.

This book provides profiles of twenty-five great West Indian cricketers along with their career highlights and statistics.

From Challenor, Constantine and Headley, through Walcott, Weekes and Worrell, Lloyd, Richards and Marshall to Lara, you are bound to find your favourite cricketer in this book.

Whether you agree with the authors' choice of the twenty-five or not, all cricket lovers will appreciate having this book, superbly illustrated with the photographs of Gordon Brooks and other noted photographers, as a souvenir of the seventy-fifth anniversary of West Indies Test cricket.

The Barbadian authors, Tony King, insurance broker and former player and cricket administrator, and Peter Laurie, writer and former Barbados ambassador, also provide a lively introduction in the novel form of a provocative dialogue about the history and sociology of West Indies cricket and their speculations about the current state of the game. There is no doubt that West Indies cricket has been going through tough times since the mid-nineties with a certain amount of uncertainty and confusion in the administration of the game. It also appears that insularity, the bane of West Indies cricket, may have had a role in the misfortunes of recent West Indies teams.

But I have no doubt that, despite the attraction of other sports, we still have a lot of talented youngsters playing the game of cricket today throughout the region.

Fortunately the selectors have recently taken the bold step of blooding these young players. I'm convinced that if they persist with this policy, complemented by proper coaching, we shall see West Indies, in the words of calypsonian David Rudder, 'rise again like a raging fire'.

For West Indians cricket is more than just a game, it is a source of national pride.

Our youngsters will find many a useful role model to emulate in the pages of THE GLORY DAYS, a valuable addition to the cricket literature of the Caribbean.

The two calypsos, 'Victory Calypso' by Lord Beginner, and David Rudder's 'Rally Round the West Indies', are the two most famous homages to cricket in song. The poem 'Rites' by the Barbadian poet, Kamau Brathwaite, is a brilliant ode to the meaning of cricket in our popular culture.

Beginner's 'Victory Calypso', or, as most people probably remember it from the first line, 'Cricket, lovely Cricket', was written to celebrate the historic West Indies victory over England at Lord's in 1950, the first time the West Indies had defeated England in a Test in England. It was the coming of age of West Indies cricket.

Rudder's 'Rally Round the West Indies' has become the unofficial anthem of West Indies cricket. It celebrates the West Indies' era of supremacy under Lloyd and Richards from 1976, laments the subsequent decline, and expresses the conviction that the West Indies will rise again 'like a raging fire'. The calypso leaves no doubt as to the seminal importance of cricket to our Caribbean nation.

'Rites' captures with wry humour the popular passion for and ambivalent attitudes to cricket of the West Indian people. Although written decades ago, it sends a timely message about the fickleness of the West Indies cricket fan in our present plight. In the words of the refrain: 'When things goin' good, you cahn touch we; but leh murder start an' ol' man, you cahn fine a man to hole up de side.'

VICTORY CALYPSO
EGBERT MOORE ('LORD BEGINNER')

Cricket lovely Cricket,
At Lord's where I saw it;
Cricket lovely Cricket,
At Lord's where I saw it;
Yardley tried his best
But Goddard won the test.
They gave the crowd plenty fun;
Second Test and West Indies won.

Chorus:
With those two little pals of mine
Ramadhin and Valentine.

The King was there well attired,
So they started with Rae and Stollmeyer;
Stolly was hitting balls around the boundary;
But Wardle stopped him at twenty.
Rae had confidence,
So he put up a strong defence;
He saw the King was waiting to see,
So he gave him a century.

Chorus:
With those two little pals of mine
Ramadhin and Valentine.

West Indies first innings total was three-twenty-six
Just as usual
When Bedser bowled Christiani
The whole thing collapsed quite easily;
England then went on,
And made one-hundred-fifty-one;
West Indies then had two-twenty lead
And Goddard said, 'That's nice indeed.'

Chorus:
With those two little pals of mine
Ramadhin and Valentine.

Yardley wasn't broken-hearted
When the second innings started;
Jenkins was like a target
Getting the first five in his basket.
But Gomez broke him down,
While Walcott licked them around;
He was not out for one-hundred and sixty-eight,
Leaving Yardley to contemplate.

Chorus:
The bowling was superfine
Ramadhin and Valentine.

West Indies was feeling homely,
Their audience had them happy.
When Washbrook's century had ended,
West Indies voices all blended.
Hats went in the air.
They jumped and shouted without fear;
So at Lord's was the scenery
Bound to go down in history.

Chorus:
After all was said and done
Second Test and the West Indies won.

RALLY ROUND THE WEST INDIES
DAVID RUDDER

For ten long years
We ruled the cricket world
Now the rule seems coming to an end
But down here
Just a chink in the armour
Is enough, enough to lose a friend
Some of the old generals have retired and gone
And the runs don't come by as they did before
But when the Toussaints go the Dessalines come
We've lost the battle but yet we will win the war

Chorus:
Rally, rally round the West Indies
Now and forever
Rally, rally round the West Indies
Never say never
Pretty soon the runs are going to flow like water
Bringing so much joy to every son and daughter
Say we're going to rise again like a raging fire
As the sun shines you know we gonna take it higher
Rally, rally round the West Indies
Now and forever
Rally, rally round the West Indies

Way Down Under a warrior falls
Michael Holding falls in the heat of the battle
'Michael shoulda left long time!'
I heard an angry brother shout
Caribbean man, that, that, that is the root of
our trouble
In these tiny theatres of conflict and confusion
Better known as the isles of the West Indies
We already know who brought us here
And who created this confusion
So I'm begging, begging my people please

Chorus...

Now they are making restrictions and laws to
spoil our beauty
But in the end we shall prevail
This is not just cricket, this thing goes beyond
the boundary
It's up to you and me to make sure that they fail
Soon we must take a side or be lost in the rubble
In a divided world that don't need islands no more
Are we doomed forever to be at somebody's mercy?
Little keys can open up mighty doors...

Chorus...

RITES
KAMAU BRATHWAITE

Many a time I have seen him savin'
the side (the tailor was saying
as he sat and sewed in his shop).

You remember that tourney wid Brandon?
What-he-name-now
that big-able water policeman-

de one in charge o' de Harbour Patrol...
You mean Hop-
a-long Cass? Is because a cow

give he mother a kick before he did born
that he foot come out so.
Yes, I know

but is not what I talkin' about.
Ol' Hoppy was bowlin' that day
as if he was hurricane father.

Lambert went in, play-
in' he know all about it as us'al
an' *swoosh!* there he go fan-

nin' outside the off-stump
an' is *click!*
he snick

de ball straight into de slips.
'Well boys it look like we lossin'
this match', says the skipper,

writin' nought in the exercise book
he was keepin' the score in; 'you think
we could chance it an' sen' Gullstone in

before Charlie or Spooks?'
So Gullstone went in.
You could see he face whitenin'

under he tan an' you know
that saga-boy frighten: bat
tappin', feet walkin' 'bout like they talkin'

wid ants; had was to stop meself axin'
meself if he ever play cricket on Brown's beach before.
An' I tole him,

I tole him over an' over
agen: *watch de ball, man,* watch
de ball like it hook to you eye

when you first goes in an' you doan know de pitch.
Uh doan mean to *poke*
but you jest got to *watch what you doin';*

this isn't no time for playin'
the fool nor makin' no sport; this is cricket!
But Gullstone too deaf:

mudder doan clean out de wax in 'e ear!
Firs' ball from Cass an' he fishin';
secon' ball an' he missin', swishin'

he bat like he wishin'
to catch butterfly;
though the all Gullstone ever could catch
pun dis beach was a cole!

But is always the trouble wid we:
too 'fraid an' too frighten.
Is all very well when it rosy an' sweet,

but leh murder start an' *bruggalungdung!*
you cahn fine a man to hole up de side.

Look wha' happen las' week at de O-val!

At de Oval?
Wha' happen las' week at de Oval?

You mean to say that you come
in here wid dat lime-skin cone

that you callin' a hat
pun you head, an' them slip slop shoe strap

on to you foot like a touris';
you sprawl you ass

all over my chair widdout ask-
in' me please leave nor licence,

wastin' muh time when you know very well that uh cahn
fine enough to finish these zoot suits

'fore Christmas; an' on top
o' all this, you could wine up de nerve to stop

me cool cool cool in de middle
o' all me needle

an' t'read; make me prick me hand in me haste;
an' tell me broad an' bole to me face

THAT YOU DOAN REALLY KNOW WHA' HAPPEN
at Kensington Oval?

We was *only* playin' de MCC, man; M-C-C
who come all de way out from Inglan.

We was battin', you see;
score wasn't too bad; one
hurren an' ninety-

seven fuh three.
The openers out, Tae Worrell out,
Everton Weekes jus' glide two fuh fifty

an' jack, is de GIANT to come!
Feller name Wardle
was bowlin'; tossin' it up

sweet sweet slow-medium syrup.
Firs' ball...
N...o...o...'

back down de wicket to Wardle.
Secon' ball...
'N...o...o...'

back down de wicket to Wardle.
Third ball comin' up
an' we know wha' goin' happen to syrup:

Clyde back pun he back
foot an' *prax!*
is through extra cover an' four red runs all de way.

'You see dat shot?' the people was shoutin';
'Jesus Chrise, man, wunna see dat shot?'
All over de groun' fellers shakin' hands wid each other

as if *they* wheelin' de willow
as if was *them* had the power;
one man run out pun de field wid a red fowl cock

goin' quawk quawk quawk in 'e han';
would'a give it to Clyde right then an' right there
if a police hadn't stop 'e!

An' in front o' where I was sittin',
one ball-headed sceptic snatch hat off he head
as if he did crazy

an' pointin' he finger at Wardle,
he jump up an' down
like a sun-shatter daisy an' bawl

out: 'B...L...O...O...D,   B...I...G   B...O...Y
bring me he B...L...O...O...D'
Who would'a think that for twenty-

five years he was standin' up there
in them Post Office cages, lickin' gloy
pun de Gover'ment stamps.

If uh wasn't there to see fuh meself,
I would'a never believe it,
I would'a never believe it.

But I say it once an' I say it agen:
when things goin' good, you cahn touch we;
but leh murder start an'
you cahn fine a man to hole up de side.

Like when Laker come on.
Goin' remember what happenin' then
for the rest o' me life.

This Laker a quiet tall heavy-face fellow
who before he start to do anything ser'ous
is hitch up he pants round he belly.

He bowlin' off-breaks.
Int makin' no fuss
jus' toss up de firs'

one an' *bap!*
Clyde play forward firm
an' de ball hit he pad

an' fly up over de wicket.
Boy, *dis* is cricket!
Laker shift weight

an' toss up de secon';
It pitchin' off-stump an' comin' back sharp
wid de men in de leg trap shinin' like shark.

Clyde stretchin' right out like a man in de dark
an' he kill it.
'N...o...o...o', from de schoolboys, 'hit it, hit it'.

Boy, dis is cricket.
Then Laker come down wid de third
one. He wrap up de ball in de palm

o' he han' like a package
AN' MAKE CLYDE WALCOTT LOOK FOOLISH.
Mister man, could'a hear

all de flies that was buzzin' out there
round de bread carts; could'a hear
if de empire fart.

An' then blue murder start:
'Kill one o' dem, Clyde', some wise-
wun was shoutin', 'knock he skull off;

doan let them tangle you up in no leg trap;
use de feet dat God give you!'
Ev'ry blabber mout' talkin',

ev'ry man jack givin' advice;
but we so frighten now at what happenin' there
we could piss we pants if we doan have a care.

'Swing de bat, man,' one feller was shoutin';
an' Clyde swing de bat but de bat miss
de ball an' de ball hit he pad

an' he pad went *biff*
like you beatin' bed
an' de empire han' stick

in de air
like Francis who dead
an' de bess o' we batsmen out.

The crowd so surprise you int hearin' a shout.
Ev'ry mout loss.
But I say it once an' I say it agen:

when things goin' good, you cahn touch
we; but leh murder start
an ol' man, you cahn fine a man to hole up de side...

INTRODUCTION

BY TONY KING AND PETER LAURIE

PETER LAURIE: Tony, let's start with the question, why this book at this time? What's so fascinating about identifying the twenty-five greatest West Indian cricketers of all time?

TONY KING: Well, Peter, the year 2003 marked the seventy-fifth anniversary of West Indies' entry into Test cricket. I think it's timely that we document the outstanding performances of a select group of our players. One could have looked at fifty or seventy-five players, but by selecting twenty-five we've kept the focus on excellence in every department of the game.

Moreover, our cricket morale is the lowest it has been for many years and both fans and our young cricketers need a reminder of where our cricket once stood and where we should be aiming to take it within the next few years. There are promising signs.

PL: It's also necessary to remind our young people that cricket is much more than a game for us in the Caribbean. For West Indians it's one of the ways in which we define ourselves as a people.

TK: Absolutely right. The youngsters today are heirs to a great and noble tradition. They truly stand on the shoulders of giants. And they must understand that; because their awareness of that, more than anything else, is the beginning of our rise again to the top.

PL: Let's deal with the choices of the twenty-five greats. You're very much a traditionalist, I'm a modernist. Yet we agreed fairly easily on the twenty-five.

First I think we should make it clear that we're not picking an expanded 'dream' team, so there's no reason to have balance in all categories. We're simply picking the best in any category. We also decided that we wouldn't let the computer choose them, i.e. we wouldn't put together a set of

statistical criteria, like number of Tests played, averages and so on. We decided to use our subjective judgment, however flawed.

Now some pick themselves. No one is going to argue over Headley, the three 'W's (Walcott, Weekes and Worrell), Sobers or Richards. Even so, you'll never get agreement on all the choices. Some are bound to be controversial. I can hear someone ask, how come Challenor? Or why Constantine over Martindale? Ramadhin and not Valentine? Desmond Haynes before Roy Fredericks? Jeffrey Dujon over Jackie Hendriks?

TK: Naturally we've had to omit a few players who've stood out over the years. Take, for example, Roy Fredericks, Charlie Griffith, Alf Valentine, Colin Croft, among others. But somebody had to fall by the wayside. In my judgment these are the top twenty-five.

We also used a historical perspective. Even if they hadn't been the great players they were, you couldn't imagine a book on West Indies cricket that didn't include Challenor and Constantine. Besides, half the fun in selecting a top twenty-five is provoking discussions over who to include and who to leave out.

PL: Anyway, there's only one cricketer you and I had difficulty in agreeing to leave out of the charmed circle of twenty-five. How do you justify the exclusion of Lawrence Rowe? Perhaps I'm prejudiced, but I was privileged to watch his magical, majestic, chanceless 302 in its entirety at Kensington in 1972. He was a magnificent batsman.

Authors Tony King and Peter Laurie

TK: Rowe was pure joy to watch. But don't forget his purple patch didn't last very long. I agree he was a fine player on his day, but he failed to fulfil all the promise he showed early in his career. And then injuries and illness didn't help either.

PL: OK, let's talk a little about the meaning of cricket for West Indians. First of all, it's always been a puzzle to many how cricket, that most English of games that has mystified outsiders - the American comedian, Robin Williams, once described it as baseball on Valium - could have appealed so strongly to the Caribbean personality.

TK: I believe our whole psychological make-up was suited to cricket. Qualities like patience, tenacity, and determination we had in fair measure.

The Sir Garfield Sobers Statue located in Barbados, West Indies

PL: It obviously struck some chord, or met some deep-seated need in Caribbean society to have caught on the way it did. In fact, no other sport or event has managed to fire the imagination of the West Indian people - of all ethnicities, colours, religions, classes, age groups and sexes - as much as a West Indies cricket match. West Indies cricket is one thing that unites West Indians.

Remember C.L.R. James on Sir Garfield Sobers: 'All geniuses are merely people who carry to an extreme definitive the characteristics of the unit of civilization to which they belong... There is embodied in him the whole history of the British West Indies.'

TK: It's interesting that Sir Garry came from among the masses and not the elite in Caribbean society. He carried with him the ambitions of so many of our people; he typified the path from humble beginnings to the very pinnacle of achievement. This should really be used as an inspiration for the whole region.

Also, I feel that we took to the game because instinctively we might have been craving something to unify the Caribbean in the early part of the twentieth century and cricket did just that. It also gave us a chance to stand alongside the bigger countries with equal status.

The importance of cricket is reflected in the fact that for West Indians our national icons are mainly cricketing icons.

Cricket was very much caught up in the issues of race, class and colonialism that typified Caribbean societies. The evolution of cricket in the Caribbean is the triumph of merit, character and justice over privilege, wealth and snobbery. James got it exactly right in *Beyond a Boundary:* 'An investigation of Worrell, Walcott and Weekes would tell us as much about the past and future of the people of the West Indies as about cricket.'

PL: Didn't the great Barbadian fast bowler, Herman Griffith, say something to the effect that without cricket blacks and whites in Barbados would have long since eaten each other?

TK: You better believe it. And it's also why that great and first in a long line of brilliant strokemakers, George Challenor, despite playing for one of the most snobbish and elitist of white clubs at the time, was respected and admired by the Barbadian masses. Professor Keith Sandiford has pointed out that Barbados, for example, has for a long time been governed by two addictions: education and cricket. So powerful are these impulses that Barbadians have never been able to disentangle them. This obsession with cricket and education sometimes transcended matters of class and race in a community that was otherwise notoriously ridden with race and class prejudice.

PL: I also think that West Indies cricket perfectly illustrates a central feature of the Caribbean personality: the ability to take an imported custom and transform it to our own purposes. Cricket and carnival - in all its various manifestations - are two central cultural facts of our creolised Caribbean identity.

TK: True. They're both necessary for our psychological well-being.

PL: Alright, but let me play devil's advocate here...

TK: ...When don't you?

PL: ...if we West Indians need supremacy at cricket to bolster our national self-esteem, then maybe that says something about the fragility of our self-esteem.

TK: My friend, if our self-esteem is fragile, then so is that of every other nation. There's no country that wouldn't like to dominate whatever sport it was good at. Think of Brazil and football...

PL: ...or Canadians and ice-hockey.

TK: Right. Really we're no exception. Remember what the West Indian writer, Ian McDonald, said, 'It is important to be the best in the world - at cricket as at anything else. It is simplistic and shallow-minded to say or think that cricket is just a game and therefore to lead the way in it means little.'

PL: That reminds me of a similar observation by the Australian writer, Thomas Keneally: 'Cricket was the great way out of Australian cultural ignominy. No Australian had ever written *Paradise Lost,* but Bradman had made 100 before lunch at Lord's.' You're right, Tony. It's no coincidence that our most popular and only living National Hero is the Right Excellent Sir Garfield Sobers.

TK: Precisely.

PL: Tony, you've been a player and manager yourself. How would you define the essence or style of West Indian cricket, the approach, attitude or technique that distinguishes it from other nations, that makes it unique?

TK: We always had a certain flair, a joie de vivre, which, when mixed with our athleticism, produced uniqueness. It's a combination of vigour, spontaneity and agility. You must remember that in the early years we played more for fun than anything else. But that changed over time. Still, we always seemed to enjoy what we were doing. I hope that quality never leaves our cricket.

PL: But doesn't that lead to the stereotype of the happy-go-lucky 'calypso' cricketer who entertains but doesn't win?

TK: Not at all. But I'm glad you raised that issue, because now we're in the doldrums there are some persons advocating that we adopt the English or Australian approaches and styles. I think that would be a fatal mistake.

Each nation has its distinctive style. What typifies ours is a naturally aggressive and elegant stroke play with strong use of the wrists, hostile fast bowling and a tiger-like grace in the field. Also the sheer inventiveness we bring to the game.

When we dominated the world in the Clive Lloyd era we did not depart from our natural style of cricket. The difference was our discipline and team spirit and our strategic and technical superiority; but our natural ebullience and inventiveness were there all the time.

The great Constantine was spot on when he observed long ago that, 'We shall never be able to play cricket in the style that it is played by so many Englishmen and now a few Australians and it is my firm belief that we can learn the atmosphere of Test cricket, get together as a side in order to pull our full weight and yet, as a side, preserve the naturalness and ease which distinguish our game.'

PL: And it was the dean of cricket writers, Neville Cardus, who commented that, 'Constantine is a representative man: he is West Indian cricket… When we see Constantine bat or bowl or field, we know he is not an English player, not an Australian player, not a South African player.'

TK: Correct. You see many people fail to appreciate that cricket is as much an intellectual as a physical activity that requires a lot of thought and practice. Brawn alone will not get you that far.

PL: What do you think are the reasons for a very small region like the West Indies producing so many world-class cricketers? The English cricket commentator, E.W. Swanton, in 1985 marvelled that '…a few scattered communities with a combined population roughly akin to the 3 million or so of Sydney or Melbourne should have produced a string of memorable batsmen at least equivalent to the combined output of England and Australia.'

TK: Don't forget that we had very little going for us in the early days. Cricket has always been a source of upward mobility within Caribbean society. The image that an outstanding cricketer carried in our society acted as an incentive to so many youngsters who had no real future otherwise.

We spoke earlier about the relation cricket bore to the wider society, and its role as a liberating force, as people like C.L.R James, Professors Hilary Beckles and Brian Stoddart and others have documented. We also mentioned Sobers' origins as well. Cricket gave so many a chance to improve themselves and their families and to show ultimately that 'we were people too.' Added to this was the fact that many teachers and businessmen who had come out to the colonies organised and financed the game, after realising that the physical and social conditions were ideal for its growth.

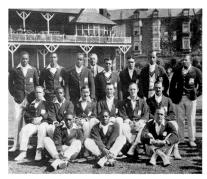

The pre-war team stars

PL: So you're saying in essence that we excel at cricket because as a people we in the Caribbean attach such importance to it?

TK: Exactly.

PL: OK, shifting the discussion somewhat, if we look at the great periods of West Indian cricket, it might be interesting to see what typifies them. First one could say that there was a prologue that began in 1923 when the West Indies team touring England performed so creditably and attractively that they definitely staked their claim to Test status. The names Challenor and Constantine immediately come to mind. What's your view of these early pioneers?

TK: Of course one also has to remember the names of those who set the whole thing up. It's not easy to call all the names but some must be mentioned here. Going back as far as 1906 we sent two fast bowlers to England, 'Floats' Woods and

The 3 'W's. Worrell, Walcott and Weekes.

Cumberbatch. Woods apparently had some difficulty bowling in boots since he was essentially a net bowler who was sponsored by one of the middle-class businessmen to whom he provided batting practice. Woods, it is alleged, asked his captain if he could remove his boots and bowl barefoot since he could not 'feel' the pitch. Folklore has it that the soles of the boots were removed to accommodate Woods.

There were people like H.B.G. Austin who led West Indies teams to England in 1900, 1906 and 1923 and who had much to do with the formation of the West Indies Cricket Board in 1927.

George Headley

Sir Pelham Warner must also be mentioned. He spent some of his formative years going to school in Trinidad and Barbados. He knew what West Indies cricket was all about and used his influence to assist the West Indies in achieving Test status.

Constantine Senior and Junior, George John, George Francis, the Grants, Nunes, along with Challenor, all played a major role in advancing the cause of West Indies cricket. The West Indies toured England in 1900, 1906 and 1923 before they were admitted to Test status in 1928 to join England and Australia, who began playing Tests in 1876-77.

George Challenor was the first in a great tradition of attacking West Indian batsmen. He was undoubtedly an influence on the three 'W's. Constantine was a brilliant all-rounder who helped to define what West Indies cricket was. In that first Test tour against England in 1928, although he didn't do so well in the actual Tests, he scored more first-class runs and took more wickets and catches than anyone else.

PL: Then there was the first period from 1928, when the West Indies were accorded Test status, to 1939, the outbreak of the Second World War. In this period there's no doubt that one genius dominated cricket, one of the greatest batsmen of all time...

TK: ...Headley, or 'Massa George' as the Jamaicans

called him, took batting to a new level in the region, and the world. If you look at his record, you'll see that no one came close to him around that period...

PL: C.L.R. James wrote 'this West Indian narrowly escapes being the greatest batsman I have ever seen. Pride of place in my list goes to Bradman, but George is not far behind.'

TK: He absorbed all the pressure put on our batting and I always wonder how we would have performed if we had two or three other quality batsmen at the time. Between 1930 and 1939 he scored ten centuries against England and Australia, while his team mates could only muster four among them.

PL: The second era began with England's tour of the Caribbean in 1947-48 after the war and ended with the series against England in the Caribbean in 1960. This was the period of the glorious batting of the incomparable three 'W's as well as the bamboozling spin of Ramadhin and Valentine - 59 wickets in four Tests between them in 1950 - and that historic first Test victory over England at Lord's as well as the equally historic series win. Yet the West Indies often suffered from inconsistency and a lack of direction in this period. In fact, after the victorious 1950 tour of England, the West Indies did not manage to win a series against England or Australia until 1963. Your thoughts on this era?

TK: You realise that by now we were becoming a real force in world cricket. The 1950 tour of England was phenomenal because of the unexpected success of two young unknown spin bowlers, Ramadhin and Valentine, and the more than expected success of Worrell, Weekes and Walcott who demolished the English bowling - Walcott and Weekes with seven centuries each and Worrell with six. The West Indies won that series 3-1.

This was the time when the various Caribbean colonies were starting to assert themselves politically and the move was on towards self-determination. The 1948 Montego Bay Conference was to lead to the West Indies Federation of 1958, which, unfortunately, survived only until 1962.

At the same time an unfortunate phenomenon became the bane of West Indian cricket - insularity. This had a negative effect on team spirit. A lot of our team prowess was diminished because everybody wanted their man as captain, and a team with most of the players from their colony. Morale was also inevitably affected by the tensions of the wider society. It was a tough time. And it showed in the 1957 tour of England when the English thrashed us 3-0. This was the period, too, when it was the norm to have a white captain regardless of merit. It was not until Worrell's appointment in 1960 as tour captain that this travesty ended.

PL: Even before Worrell, whose appointment was overdue, Constantine and Headley ought by right to have captained the West Indies for the 1933 and 1939 tours of England respectively.

TK: Of course. After the war there were more international matches and more West Indian cricketers began playing in the professional leagues in Britain. People like Constantine, the three 'W's, Sobers, and many others got valuable experience both on and off the field playing professional cricket in the leagues. To be a professional meant to be the 'star citizen' of the community especially in post-war England where people used to travel hundreds of miles on week-ends just to see these West Indian pros.

PL: Then towards the end of this era we see the emergence of Garry Sobers as the greatest cricketer of all time, and Wes Hall as a premier fast bowler, not to mention great players like Rohan Kanhai, Lance Gibbs, Conrad Hunte, Seymour Nurse, Charlie Griffith, Basil Butcher and Joe Solomon.

Bust of Sir Frank Worrell

TK: Yes, the stage was now being set for the first real dominance by the West Indies and those two and the others did play a key role in that dominance from 1962 to 1967. Remember, Garry's 365 not out came in 1958.

Queen's Park Oval, Trinidad

PL: The third period might be said to stretch from 1960 to 1974. This period began under the brilliant captaincy of Frank Worrell: 9 wins, 3 defeats, 2 draws and the famous tied Test with Australia. Not a bad record! What did you think was specifically great about Worrell as a captain?

TK: Worrell had the good fortune of being seen as a father figure to most of the players he captained. They regarded him with respect and affection. By 1960

he had acquired such vast experience in the Test arena that he was more than equipped for the job. He was a Barbadian who lived many years in Jamaica and Trinidad and understood the West Indian mind. He also understood the importance of cricket to the West Indian man in the street. He managed to unite a number of brilliant players into a cohesive, disciplined team.

The 1960-61 series against Australia gave West Indies cricket enormous international prestige. It was one of the most thrilling series ever. It saw one of Sobers' most brilliant Test innings - 132 in the first Test at Brisbane - and the consistent mastery of Rohan Kanhai. It also saw Lance Gibbs emerge as a top class spinner. The tied Test at Brisbane is part of cricket's enduring legends. That final last over has been immortalised in words by many, including our own Wes Hall, who was the bowler.

That tour, which was the first to Australia since 1951-52, also had an enduring impact on the Australian cricket public. Never before had they seen cricket as exciting as this. Half a million people turned out to see the West Indies team off at Melbourne. The series in Australia was followed by a 5-0 thrashing of India in the Caribbean in 1962 and then the hugely popular 1963 tour of England where the West Indies triumphed 3-1.

PL: This period began with Worrell and ended under the captaincy of Sobers, and for a brief spell, Kanhai. After the 1960-61 tour of Australia until 1967, West Indies did not lose a series and got their first series win against Australia in 1964-65. But from 1967 to 1975 we only managed to win two rubbers. Towards the end of the period the West Indies were a weakened team in transition with Sobers often single-handedly carrying the brunt of the batting. But tell me, Sobers is such a genius that I guess people had unrealistic expectations of him as a captain. Hence his captaincy often came in for some criticism. How do you rate him as a captain?

Sir Garfield Sobers

UWI Cricket Memorial, Barbados

TK: Sobers was a good captain. I remember a conversation I had with Sir Frank Worrell in 1963. He was of the view that if he had to leave the field for any length of time, in his absence Sobers would have carried on exactly as he wanted. Such was the confidence Worrell had in him. Maybe Sobers' problem was that he felt his players were as good as he and hence his expectations of them were too high. I think he also suffered because insularity was again a factor after 1966.

PL: Then we have the greatest period of West Indies cricket, the Lloyd and Richards era that began in 1974 and ended in the mid-1990s when the decline of the West Indies began. At the same time this triumphant era began with a shock: the humiliating 5-1 defeat of the West Indies by Australia at home in the 1975-76 series when Dennis Lillee and Jeff Thompson ripped through our team with their pace.

But after that, the West Indies dominated world cricket so completely that it seemed they could never be dislodged - twenty-eight consecutive series without a loss; the 1975 and 1979 World Cups - and almost the 1983 one. From 1975-76 to 1994-95 the West Indies lost only two of the thirty-six series they played.

What do you attribute this incredible success to? Is there a formula that can be repeated or recaptured?

TK: For me the answer is easy. The combination of six good batsmen, a wicket-keeper and four outstanding fast bowlers is the main reason why we dominated world cricket. Don't forget that it was that same disastrous tour when Lillee and Thompson routed our boys that made Lloyd decide that pace was the answer. And not just pace, but a four-pronged pace attack. This was to lead to the greatest pace attack ever that included at one time or another Roberts, Holding, Garner, Croft, Marshall, Walsh, Bishop and Ambrose.

PL: So you're saying that fast bowling is the key?

TK: Aggressive, quality fast bowling. Look, of our twenty-five great players, nine are fast bowlers, if we include Sobers. That should tell you something. No batting line-up has ever totally dominated quality fast bowling in the history of Test cricket. Remember Larwood and Voce, Lindwall and Miller, Trueman and Statham, Hall and Griffith, Lillee and Thompson, and our crop of great fast bowlers under Lloyd.

And look at the world records: most wickets - Walsh; best earned run average - Marshall. *Res ipsa loquitur.*

PL: As an aside, Tony, what about the state of pitches in the Caribbean today? Michael Holding has said that if he were playing on

these tracks today he would probably be an off-spinner.

TK: We have tended to produce batting tracks rather than tracks to assist the bowlers. OK, wicket preparation is not an exact science, but our curators could do a lot better.

PL: It also seems that under Lloyd there was a greater degree of professionalism. The West Indies were fantastic in the field.

TK: The Kerry Packer World Series experience had something to do with that, in that it moulded our boys as a team. Plus Packer insisted on discipline and professional commitment. Lloyd was able to carry that over and build on it. He definitely put his stamp on the team. We also inherited the services of Australian physiotherapist Dennis Waight, and he, more than any one else, brought a new level of fitness to our team during that period.

PL: Finally to the present era. Sadly to say, the last decade has seen the decline of West Indies cricket. Since 1995 we've managed to win only nine out of twenty-four series. The endless supply of great fast bowlers seems to have dried up - Walsh seemingly the last - and only one batsman has emerged who is indisputably a brilliant cricketer: Brian Lara. How do you rate Lara?

TK: He is obviously the most talented batsman of the modern era, including Tendulkar. The difference between the two of them is that Tendulkar is more consistent, but on his day Lara can take batting to a level that no one else can hope to achieve. Currently we have a lot of talent among our youngsters but they don't seem to have the hunger to achieve greatness.

Malcolm Marshall

Brian Lara

PL: Alright, Tony, let's get to the hot topic of the day: what are the causes of the decline of West Indies cricket since the mid-1990s? After Richards' retirement we've seen a succession of brief captaincies, turmoil in the West Indies Cricket Board, chopping and changing in team selection, endless bickering and confusion, and generally inconsistent or poor performances, including humiliating whitewashes by Australia, South Africa and Sri Lanka. What needs to be done to get us back to the top again?

TK: There are many reasons for the decline. We became very complacent and never worked hard enough to keep a constant flow of quality players on stand-by. We assumed that players would emerge from

players? I raise the management issue because there are those who feel that some of the great players of the 1980s were discarded unceremoniously and there seemed to have been no succession plan. I believe we lost Greenidge, Haynes, Marshall, Richards and Dujon all in the space of a few years. On the other hand, I doubt that we have the talent today that was around in the 1980s, at least not in the bowling or wicket-keeping departments. In addition, I've heard several Australian commentators claim that the management of their cricket is their strongest point.

some back street and dominate the world scene. But it doesn't work that way. When other teams were developing programmes for the future, we sat on our laurels. Other countries went back to the drawing board and developed a burning desire to reach the top of the heap. The Australians, for example, never forgot the Bradman legacy. We, on the other hand, seem not to have recognised that we had a great legacy to protect - Headley, the three 'W's, Sobers, to name a few. That is the essential difference in the approach of the two cricketing nations.

PL: On that point, the present Australian team is incredibly strong, as we saw in the 2003 World Cup and in the 3-1 Test series against the West Indies the same year. How would you rate them against the great West Indies teams of the Lloyd era?

TK: I admit that the Aussies have some superb players and show a high level of professionalism. They're always well prepared physically and mentally. But I would still give the edge to the Lloyd teams because of the sheer power of the bowling attack.

PL: Is the decline associated primarily with the management of West Indies cricket or with the

TK: I hate to admit it but we haven't had the best from our administrators especially in recent years. I think that some of them put their emphasis on the wrong things. One has to have the right balance between finance, players' interests, and development. From what I can see, the Aussies have done well in those areas. Moreover, they set targets and are serious about achieving them.

PL: What about the attitude of players today? Many of the greats who played for the West Indies in the late 1970s and 1980s speak of the professionalism and commitment of the team of that era. Is that missing now?

TK: That's not an easy question, you know. I'm sure the present players all feel that they are professional and committed. Unfortunately, they don't have the results to show. Besides, all these problems are more pronounced when you're losing. But we do have a lot of talented youngsters playing the game today.

PL: A big problem I see - and I hope you can tell me I'm wrong - is that there doesn't seem to be the pride and passion to succeed that previous generations of our cricketers had. When you saw Holding run in to bowl or Richards walk to the crease to bat, you knew this was not just cricket, this was war.

TK: Many of the players of that era had to work hard to reach that level. What we're seeing now in cricket is also evident in the wider society. A certain level of comfort has pervaded West Indian society and so much is laid on for us without our having to work for it.

PL: In a more pessimistic vein, youngsters today have many choices of sports other than cricket. There's also the strong American cultural influence. Isn't it possible that today's generation of West Indian youth will never care or feel about cricket the way previous generations did? Maybe - perish the thought - we will never rise again?

TK: I've argued that we haven't done much of a job in keeping cricket in the minds of our young people. Our junior programmes have lacked intensity and as a result we've allowed other sports to catch the imagination of our youngsters. We need to do a lot more work at the lower level in the primary and secondary school systems. Again, we've taken too much for granted. But I'm not pessimistic at all about the future of the game.

PL: The great players of the past almost to a man played professional cricket in England or Australia. Today's young West Indian cricketers either don't have or don't take up this option. Some have suggested that this may be a factor in the decline, the lack of professional opportunities. On the other hand, New Zealand is doing well, and most of their players, as far as I know, don't play professionally. Should we, and can we have a professional league in the Caribbean? And what about the coaching and training at all levels?

TK: We seem to have no alternative but to have a professional league in the Caribbean. That, however, will require substantial funding, and where will that come from? I can't see a league maintaining itself, unfortunately. With the overseas opportunities being non-existent, our players have suffered because we play too little first-class cricket but I still feel that we can do better if we make the necessary mental adjustment.

As for coaching I'm not satisfied with the consistency of our programmes. Every now and then, a clinic is put on but some argue that the money is lacking to really push meaningful development.

PL: Tony, some final reflections on cricket in general today. I know purists like yourself think that the One-Day game is the worst thing that ever happened to cricket.

I happen to think it's a great thing. I think we owe a great deal to Packer for injecting some excitement into the game. There have been innings of elegance from great batsmen in One-Day games. It's not all slog and swipe. And at least you are guaranteed a result, and more often than not, a very exciting finish. I find it hard at times to be enthusiastic about a game that lasts five days and ends in a boring draw. I'm all for 'glorious uncertainties' but I like a result. Let me ask you first, assuming that One-Day cricket is here to stay, are there any modifications you would like to see to the game?

TK: You know very well that I'm not much of a One-Day fan. I grew up steeped in the tradition of the longer game, and its beauty and intrigue can't be matched by the shorter version. Sorry, Pete, but I can live without One-Day cricket.

As for modifications they've made so many already that there is no need for further changes.

PL: So on to the next question, are there any modifications to Test cricket that might inject more excitement into the game without ruining it for a traditionalist like you? For example, what about a match lasting two days with 100 overs per innings? Or, if you wish, lasting four days with two innings of 100 overs each? Is there anything that Test cricket could usefully borrow from the One-Day variant of the game?

TK: I want to see Test cricket remain as it is. Those who love the traditional game will still come out and watch it for all the same reasons. If you change it too much, then it wouldn't be cricket. So leave my Test cricket alone!

PL: So don't tell me you disapprove of the use of technology to help umpires? Surely that could even be extended - for example, using the third umpire to determine whether the ball hit the bat before the pad in an LBW decision or whether the ball touched the bat or gloves in a catch?

TK: I'm very much a traditionalist and still like to see the control of the game in the hands of competent standing umpires. If too much technology creeps in, all the lore and interest that have been the stuff of cricket legends will be diminished. Much of the fascination of the game will go.

PL: Tony, what about sportsmanship today? Cricket is in many ways the epitome of sportsmanship, as in the expression 'it's not cricket' to refer to cheating or something similarly unacceptable. Sobers was famous for walking if he edged the ball and it had been caught. Brian Lara today has that reputation, but they appear to be a dying breed.

Let me play devil's advocate and argue that batsmen should leave the umpires to do their job and should on no account walk before they're given out. Besides, the umpiring is so atrocious today, why help them? The Australians play the game hard, and I suspect any Australian batsmen who walked without having been given out, or a fielder who signalled that he had not taken a clean catch, might be disciplined by the team management. What do you think?

TK: I still think we have to see honesty in the game, but if there's any doubt in any player's mind as to whether someone is out or not it should be left to the umpire to decide.

PL: We touched on management earlier when we were talking about the possible causes of the decline of West Indies cricket, but I'd like to come back to it in a more general way.

Cricket today is like negotiation. And 90 per cent of good negotiation is preparation. It seems to me that the team that has done a thorough analysis of the game of each member of the opposing team is better prepared to win. In this context, don't you think that the relative roles of the captain and the manager/coach could be adjusted? I'm thinking here of baseball where it is the manager who makes all the strategic and even tactical decisions. Might it not be better to leave all the strategic decisions (whether to bat first; if and when to declare etc)

captain it - as the captaincy is presently understood. Worrell and Lloyd are brilliant exceptions. It might be much easier to find a brilliant manager/coach than a brilliant captain. Your thoughts?

TK: Peter, don't you try to Americanise my cricket! Cricket has thrived on tradition and uniqueness. For God's sake, don't change that! Cricketers would be like robots if you bring about the changes you mentioned. If we do the right things from the early stages, it would be easy to create leaders.

PL: I think that Caribbean governments have a responsibility to put cricket on a sound financial footing in partnership with the regional private sector. This, after all, is not just any sport: this is a key part of our culture. If we allow cricket to wither and die, we lose our soul. If regional governments can help fund and oversee the development of our carnival festivals, they can surely do the same for cricket. I think we have reached the stage where the fortunes of West Indian cricket can no longer be left to the West Indies Cricket Board; some new structure for the administration of cricket must be put in place; one that has greater accountability.

TK: I'll agree that a common effort must be made by all parties, but as you know when politicians assist with funding they like to know that they have some control. A competent Board along with private and public sector funding in theory can do the job.

PL: Alright Tony, finally, do you think there is a chance that West Indies will rise again 'like a raging fire' to quote David Rudder?

Kensington Oval, Bridgetown, Barbados

and even some of the tactical decisions (who to bowl, what field to set) to the manager/coach, who has a more detached perspective of the game from the pavilion, and leave the captain to concentrate on keeping up the spirits and concentration of his team mates on the field? We keep on agonising in the Caribbean about finding a good captain. But not all players who have the skill to play on the team have the intellectual skills to

TK: My only concern is whether we have the will to dominate world cricket again. If so, and we put the right developmental programmes in place, I can see us returning to the glory days. Let's face it; it's not an easy job. And all the forces in West Indies cricket must be working hand in hand to achieve the same thing. Let's hope we see it in our lifetime.

PROFILES IN GLORY - ALPHABETICAL LIST

NAME	PLACE OF BIRTH	DATE OF BIRTH	
CURTLY ELCONN LYNWALL **AMBROSE**	ANTIGUA	21.09.63	
GEORGE **CHALLENOR**	BARBADOS	28.06.1888	(DECEASED 30.07.47)
LEARIE NICHOLAS **CONSTANTINE**	TRINIDAD	21.09.01	(DECEASED 01.07.71)
PETER JEFFREY LEROY **DUJON**	JAMAICA	28.05.56	
JOEL **GARNER**	BARBADOS	16.12.52	
LANCELOT RICHARD **GIBBS**	GUYANA	29.09.34	
CUTHBERT GORDON **GREENIDGE**	BARBADOS	01.05.51	
WESLEY WINFIELD **HALL**	BARBADOS	12.09.39	
DESMOND LEO **HAYNES**	BARBADOS	15.02.56	
GEORGE ALPHONSO **HEADLEY**	PANAMA	30.05.09	(DECEASED 30.11.83)
MICHAEL ANTHONY **HOLDING**	JAMAICA	16.02.54	
CONRAD CLEOPHAS **HUNTE**	BARBADOS	09.05.32	(DECEASED 03.12.99)
ALVIN ISAAC **KALLICHARRAN**	GUYANA	21.03.49	
ROHAN BHOLALLAL **KANHAI**	GUYANA	26.12.35	
BRIAN CHARLES **LARA**	TRINIDAD	02.05.69	
CLIVE HUBERT **LLOYD**	GUYANA	31.08.44	
MALCOLM DENZIL **MARSHALL**	BARBADOS	18.04.58	(DECEASED 04.11.99)
K.T. SONNY **RAMADHIN**	TRINIDAD	01.05.29	
ISAAC VIVIAN ALEXANDER **RICHARDS**	ANTIGUA	07.03.52	
ANDERSON MONTGOMERY EVERTON **ROBERTS**	ANTIGUA	29.01.51	
GARFIELD ST. AUBRUN **SOBERS**	BARBADOS	28.07.36	
CLYDE LEOPOLD **WALCOTT**	BARBADOS	17.01.26	
COURTNEY ANDREW **WALSH**	JAMAICA	30.10.62	
EVERTON DE COURCY **WEEKES**	BARBADOS	26.02.25	
FRANK MORTIMER MAGLINNE **WORRELL**	BARBADOS	01.08.24	(DECEASED 13.03.67)

THE
EARLY

YEARS

1923-39

THE WEST INDIES WERE GRANTED TEST STATUS IN 1928,

LARGELY ON THE BASIS OF THE BRILLIANT PERFORMANCES

OF TWO WEST INDIAN TRAILBLAZERS ON THE 1923 TOUR

OF ENGLAND, GEORGE CHALLENOR AND LEARIE

CONSTANTINE. THESE GREAT PIONEERS WERE FOLLOWED

BY THE GENIUS WHO DOMINATED WEST INDIES CRICKET IN

THE 1930S: GEORGE HEADLEY

GEORGE CHALLENOR

BARBADOS

George Challenor's inclusion in any list of twenty-five great West Indies cricketers obviously cannot rest on his Test record.

He played in only three Tests in the first series after the West Indies were granted Test status - the humbling 1928 tour of England when the West Indies came up against the full might of England (Hobbs, Sutcliffe, Hammond, Tate and Larwood to name but a few) and lost all three matches by an innings. But by then Challenor was 41 and but a shadow of the master batsman that he had been.

Challenor's claim rests on his being the first in a line of great West Indies batsmen. As the cricket historian Professor Keith Sandiford has said, 'Challenor was born rich and batted like a millionaire' He was an aggressive and brilliant strokemaker with a technically sound defence. He started the tradition of what came to be identified as West Indian batsmanship and provided inspiration for so many young players like the three 'W's - Walcott, Weekes and Worrell - who took batting to a new level.

His first-class statistics are therefore a more accurate reflection of his talent: 5,822 runs at an average of 38.55, including fifteen centuries.

As C.L.R. James said of him, 'Challenor symbolised batting, in every hovel and palace in the Caribbean.'

Challenor was the first cricketer to have a pavillion named after him at Kensington Oval in Barbados.

CAREER HIGHLIGHTS

Unfortunately, Challenor's greatest innings were made prior to the West Indies being accorded Test status in 1928. By then, he was past his cricketing prime. Even so, in the inaugural Test series against England in 1928, Challenor made an impressive 46 against the fast and hostile bowling of Harold Larwood in the third and final Test at The Oval.

Some of his greatest innings were made playing for Barbados and for the West Indies before Test status was achieved.

He opened the batting for Barbados consistently between 1920 and 1927 with Tim Tarilton, a pair that later Gordon Greenidge and Desmond Haynes would emulate. In one inter-territorial tournament they produced an opening stand of 183 against British Guiana, with Challenor making 105. In a match against Trinidad they shared in an opening partnership of 292, with Challenor making a brilliant 220. In all Challenor scored six centuries in ten innings.

On the 1906 tour of England when he was only 18 he already impressed those who saw him. Against an English team touring the West Indies in 1912 he scored two centuries. But it was on the 1923 tour of England that Challenor's extraordinary talent became evident for all to see. There is no doubt that it was Challenor's batting, along with the achievements of the superb all-rounder Learie Constantine, that proved that the West Indies were worthy of being accorded Test status - which they were granted in 1928. On that tour Challenor scored 1,556 first class runs, including six centuries, at an average of 61, and was considered by *Wisden* to be among the six finest batsmen in the world at the time. CLR James, Herman Griffith and Constantine all considered him the greatest of his generation. This included batsmen of the calibre of Hobbs, Suttcliffe, Hendren, Macartney and Woolley. Indeed, he was third in the English batting averages that summer.

CAREER STATISTICS

George Challenor • Barbados • 1888-1947 • Right-hand batsman • Right-arm medium bowler
Test debut: v. England at Lord's, 1928

TESTS

Batting & Fielding	M	I	NO	Runs	HS	Ave	100	50	Ct	St
	3	6	0	101	46	16.83	0	0	0	0

Bowling	O	M	R	W	Ave	BBI	5	10	SR	Econ
	-	-	-	-	-	-	-	-	-	-

FIRST-CLASS (1905/06-1929/30)

Batting & Fielding	M	I	NO	Runs	HS	Ave	100	50	Ct	St
	95	160	9	5822	237*	38.55	15	29	25	0

Bowling	Balls	M	R	W	Ave	BBI	5	10	SR	Econ
	2619	93	1290	54	23.88	4-16	0	0	48.5	2.95

SIR
NICHOLAS LEARIE CONSTANTINE

BARON OF MARAVAL AND NELSON

TRINIDAD

Nicholas Learie Constantine merits inclusion in any list of great West Indies cricketers if only for the fact that his achievements paved the way for the West Indies' accession to Test status.

Learie Constantine was one of the early cricketers from the West Indies who received widespread popular acclaim as one of those who helped to chart the course of West Indian cricket, both as a brilliant all-rounder and an ambassador for the region. When people speak of a characteristic West Indian style of cricket, it is Constantine who defined it. His enthusiasm and competitiveness, along with an intellectual grasp of the subtleties of, and sheer delight in, the game have come over the years to typify the tradition of West Indian cricket.

As a young man, Constantine was as quick as any other fast bowler. Later he would vary his pace to great effect. He was a superb fielder at any position, anticipating with unerring accuracy where the batsman would hit the ball and making spectacular catches. Later in life, Sir Learie related how one day he had difficulty in taking a particular batsman's wicket since the slip fielders were dropping all the catches. He said to himself, 'Constantino, if he is going to be done in today, you will have to do it all alone. So I went back to my mark, ran in and bowled him an out-swinger which predictably hit the outside edge and there was I at gully to take the catch!'

He was a specialist at coverpoint. He took 133 catches in 117 first-class matches, and 28 catches in 18 Tests. But his Test statistics don't tell the true story. He took 58 wickets at an average of 30.10 and made 635 runs at an average of 19.24 in 18 Tests. His first-class figures are more revealing: 4,451 runs at an average of 24.32, and 424 wickets at an average of 20.61.

Constantine was *Wisden* Cricketer of the Year in 1940. *Wisden* commented, 'A cricketer who will never be forgotten, who took great heed that all nature's gifts should be, as it were, expanded by usage, a deep thinker and an athlete whose every movement was a joy to behold.' Constantine pursued a distinguished career in law, politics and diplomacy after he gave up cricket. He consistently fought for the rights of black people in the United Kingdom. He was elected to the Trinidad Parliament in 1956 and was appointed a government minister.

In 1962 he was knighted, and served as his country's High Commissioner in the United Kingdom from 1962 to 1964. Following that he held many distinguished positions in the UK.

Sir Learie was created a life peer in 1969, Lord Constantine of Maraval and Nelson, the first peerage for a person of African descent.

Lord Constantine died in 1971, and was posthumously awarded Trinidad & Tobago's highest honour, the Trinity Cross.

He was the author of six books on cricket.

CAREER HIGHLIGHTS

Learie first toured England as a young man in 1923. His versatility was immediately evident. Masterful in the field, he also captured 37 wickets at an average of 21.86 as first or second change bowler and helped himself to some runs as well.

On the 1928 tour of England, although he did only moderately well in the Tests, he had some scintillating performances against County sides. He was the leading wicket-taker with 107 at an average of 22.95, the leading batsman with 1,381 runs at an average of 34.52, and took 29 catches.

Against the mighty Middlesex team he top-scored in the first innings with a hurricane 86 (50 from four overs in 18 minutes!). Then he returned in the second innings to destroy the County with 7 for 57 with vicious pace and swing. To top it off, he scored another aggressive 103 in the West Indies' second innings to clinch the victory. According to *The Times*, the spectators, abandoning all English reserve, stood on their seats and applauded each thunderous stroke.

Back in the Caribbean, in 1930 he sparkled against the touring England side. In the second Test in Trinidad, he top-scored with 58. Then he took 4 for 35 and 5 for 87 in the two innings of the third Test in British Guiana, leading the West Indies to victory.

In England's 1935 tour of the Caribbean, Constantine was in his prime, and was a key factor in the West Indies winning their first Test series against England. He scored a dashing 90 and took 3 for 11 to help the West Indies win the second Test in Trinidad. In his final Test match for the West Indies against England at The Oval in 1939, Constantine took 5 for 75 and hit 79.

Constantine also excelled for Nelson in the Lancashire League from 1929 to 1937 where he scored 6,673 runs at an average of 38.35 and took 790 wickets at an average of 9.90.

Sir Nicholas Learie Constantine • Trinidad • 1901-1971 • Right-arm fast bowler • Right-hand batsman
Test debut: v. England at Lord's, 1928

TESTS

Batting & Fielding	M	I	NO	Runs	HS	Ave	100	50	Ct	St
	18	33	0	635	90	19.24	0	4	28	0

Bowling	Balls	M	R	W	Ave	BBI	5	10	SR	Econ
	3583	125	1746	58	30.10	5-75	2	0	61.7	2.92

FIRST-CLASS (1921/22-1938/39)

Batting & Fielding	M	I	NO	Runs	HS	Ave	100	50	Ct	St
	119	197	11	4475	133	24.05	5	28	133	0

Bowling	Balls	M	R	W	Ave	BBI	5	10	SR	Econ
	17393	481	8991	439	20.48	8-38	25	4	39.6	3.10

GEORGE ALPHONSO HEADLEY

JAMAICA

George Headley is considered by many to be the greatest batsman the West Indies ever produced, and one of the best batsmen in the world. He was often described as the 'black Bradman', but many West Indians of the era thought it more appropriate to describe Bradman as the 'white Headley'.

He was a compact man of medium height. His movements were precise and economical. He oozed confidence. And whether on or off the field, he was always immaculate in his dress.

He was the first West Indian to score a century on his debut. He is the only player to score four centuries before the age of 21. In 22 Tests he scored 2,190 runs, including eight centuries and two double centuries, at an average of 60.83! And that was against the full might of England and Australia. That average is exceeded only by Bradman and Graeme Pollock.

Even more extraordinary was that Headley shouldered the entire burden of the batting of what was a weak West Indies team through the 1930s, earning the nickname 'Atlas'. He returned to captain the team in the first post-war Test - the first black man to do so.

Headley had fantastic technique, playing late and keeping his head absolutely still. C.L.R. James wrote of him that he had to a superlative degree the three cardinal qualities of the super batsman: 'He saw the ball early. He was quick on his feet. He was quick with his bat.' Indeed, the secret of his batting lay in his perfect timing as he cut or drove on both sides of the wicket, and his extraordinary ability to focus on the job at hand. He was best off the back foot, where his exceptional eye and nimble footwork allowed him to play the ball unusually late and with maximum power. At the same time he had an exceptionally sound defence.

He was comfortable against all kinds of bowling, and was a superb player on sticky wickets, which were the order of the day prior to the covering of pitches. He was also a good fielder in any position.

Like Frank Worrell later, he was a fine ambassador of the game. His composure on and off the field in exceptionally trying and unjust circumstances earned him widespread respect.

After retirement Headley worked as a coach for the government of Jamaica. He died at the age of 74 in 1983. The biggest stand at Sabina cricket ground is named in his honour.

A true Caribbean man, if ever there was one, George Headley was born in Panama in 1909, a product of a Jamaican and Barbadian union, and grew up playing baseball in Cuba. He was taken to Jamaica at ten years of age and by the time he was 18 he was playing cricket for the island.

He scored 71 and 211 in two matches for Jamaica against Lord Tennyson's XI in 1927-28, when still 18. He was recognised as a sensation. But he did not play for the West Indies until 1930.

In his first Test against England in Barbados, at the age of 20, he made 21 and 171. In that magnificent innings Headley ignited the imagination and won the hearts of all Barbadians with a display of batsmanship second to none. No other Jamaican would do that until Lawrence Rowe in 1972.

In the third Test in Guyana he made 114 and 112, leading the West Indies to their first Test victory. In the final match in Jamaica he hit 223 with 28 fours. He ended his first Test series with an aggregate of 703 at an average of 87.87.

The tour of Australia in 1930-31 illustrated Headley's application to, and analysis of, the game. Headley was a fine off-side player but lacked a similar variety of strokes on the leg side. So the Australians, especially their great leg-spinner Clarrie Grimmett, began to bowl at his legs with success. In response, Headley changed his grip and stance to develop greater versatility on the leg side, and made two scintillating Test centuries after the change. He ended the tour with 1,066 first-class runs at an average of 44. By the end of the tour Grimmett himself judged him 'the finest on-side player in the world'.

Back in the Caribbean, Headley made some brilliant scores against Lord Tennyson's touring side: 344 not out, 84, 155 not out and 140. This led Tennyson to comment that he had never seen such perfect timing or variety of strokes. On the tour of England in 1933, he scored 2,320 first-class runs, including seven centuries.

In the Tests, he made 50 in the first match at Lord's and 169 not out in the second Test at Old Trafford. He ended the three-Test series with an aggregate of 277 runs at an average of 55.40.

Headley had a magnificent series against England in the Caribbean in 1934-35, culminating with a superb unbeaten 270 with 30 fours in the final Test in Jamaica, leading the West Indies to victory in the rubber. That innings has long been adjudged one of the best ever played by a West Indian. He had an aggregate of 485 in the four Tests at an average of 97.00.

The West Indies did not play Test cricket again until the tour of England in 1939. In the first Test at Lord's he scored 106 and 107. He amassed 334 runs in the three Tests at an average of 66.80.

The war deprived the cricketing world of what would have been Headley's best years. After the war he became the first black player to lead the West Indies, being appointed captain for the first Test in Barbados against England in 1947-48.

CAREER STATISTICS

George Alphonso Headley • Panama • 1909-1983 • Right-hand batsman • Right-arm leg-break bowler
Test debut: v. England at Bridgetown, 1930

TESTS

Batting & Fielding	M	I	NO	Runs	HS	Ave	100	50	Ct	St
	22	40	4	2190	270*	60.83	10	5	14	0

Bowling	Balls	M	R	W	Ave	BBI	5	10	SR	Econ
	398	7	230	0	-	-	0	0	-	3.46

FIRST-CLASS (1927/28-1953/54)

Batting & Fielding	M	I	NO	Runs	HS	Ave	100	50	Ct	St
	103	164	22	9921	344*	69.86	33	44	76	0

Bowling	Balls	M	R	W	Ave	BBI	5	10	SR	Econ
	3845	107	1842	51	36.11	5-33	1	0	75.3	2.87

THE
POST-WA

R YEARS

1947-60

THE PERIOD AFTER THE SECOND WORLD WAR SAW THE WEST

INDIES BEAT ENGLAND IN A TEST IN ENGLAND FOR THE FIRST

TIME – THE HISTORIC 1950 LORD'S TEST. THE WEST INDIES

ALSO WON THE SERIES 3-1. FROM THIS ERA COME FOUR OF THE

GREATS: RAMADHIN, WALCOTT, WEEKES AND WORRELL.

K.T.
SONNY RAMADHIN

TRINIDAD

In the history of great spin bowlers Sonny Ramadhin stands out. Ramadhin was the first East Indian to play for the West Indies, and was the first great spin bowler to emerge from the West Indies. Ramadhin and Alf Valentine were one of the first pairs of world-class spinners to operate together at Test level.

It was 'those two pals of mine', Ramadhin and Valentine, who, along with the batting of the three 'W's, were responsible for the West Indies defeating England in England for the first time in 1950, propelling West Indian cricket to a new international level.

His unorthodox grip led him to mystify many opposing batsmen. He was able to bowl both leg and off breaks using the same apparent action. This, coupled with the fact that he always bowled with sleeves buttoned at the wrist, added to his reputation for guile and magic.

But the strength of his bowling lay in his great command of line and length and his extraordinary consistency during incredibly long bowling spells (in the second innings of the first Test against England in 1957 Ramadhin sent down 774 deliveries!)
The sad fact is that Ramadhin was a victim of his own success. He was grossly overbowled, following his success against England on the 1950 tour.

Ramadhin took 158 wickets at an average of 28.98 in 43 Tests, and was *Wisden* Cricketer of the Year in 1951. After he retired, Ramadhin lived in England where he ran a successful pub in Oldham, Lancashire.

CAREER HIGHLIGHTS

A virtually unknown youngster, Ramadhin made his debut for the West Indies on the 1950 tour of England where, with Valentine, he proved to be the West Indies' trump card.

On that historic tour when the West Indies defeated England in England for the first time (3-1), Ramadhin took 135 first-class wickets at an average of 14.88, and in the four Tests 26 wickets at an average of 23.23. This included 5 for 66 in the first innings, and 6 for 86 off 72 overs in the second innings of the second Test at Lord's, to help the West Indies to their first ever Test victory in England. This was indeed a declaration of independence by the West Indian colonies. In the third Test at Trent Bridge he took 5 for 135 to lead the West Indies to another win.

After the England tour Ramadhin was a fixture in the West Indies side for over a decade. He also played in the Lancashire League in the 1950s. When England toured the Caribbean in 1953-54 he took four wickets in the first two Tests and then 6 for 113 in the third Test in Guyana. He led the wicket-takers on both sides with 23 at an average of 24.30 for the series.

On the tour of New Zealand in 1955-56, Ramadhin took 6 for 23 off 21.2 overs in the first Test at Dunedin, followed by nine wickets in the second Test at Christchurch, including 5 for 46 in the first innings. His haul for the four-game series was 22 wickets at an average of 15.80.

On the 1957 tour of England, in the first Test at Edgbaston he took 7 for 49 in 31 overs in the first innings. In the second innings he looked as if he would run through the side when Colin Cowdrey and Peter May devised a method of defence by blocking balls with their front pad. This led to a public outcry and the eventual change of the LBW rule. Ramadhin ended the series heading the bowling in first-class matches with 119 wickets at a cost of 13.98.

Ramadhin retired in 1960.

K.T. Sonny Ramadhin • Trinidad • 1929 • Right-arm off-break bowler • Right-hand batsman
Test debut: v. England at Old Trafford, 1950

TESTS

Batting & Fielding	M	I	NO	Runs	HS	Ave	100	50	Ct	St
	43	58	14	361	44	8.20	0	0	9	0

Bowling	Balls	M	R	W	Ave	BBI	5	10	SR	Econ
	13939	813	4579	158	28.98	7-49	10	1	88.2	1.97

FIRST-CLASS (1949/50-1965)

Batting & Fielding	M	I	NO	Runs	HS	Ave	100	50	Ct	St
	184	191	65	1092	44	8.66	0	0	38	0

Bowling	Balls	M	R	W	Ave	BBI	5	10	SR	Econ
	-	-	15345	758	20.24	8-15	51	15	59.2	2.04

SIR
CLYDE LEOPOLD WALCOTT

BARBADOS

Clyde Leopold Walcott was a prodigiously talented cricketer and a superstar of a batsman, one of the immortal three 'W's who dominated cricket in the 1950s.

Tall (6'2") and with a powerful physique, he was one of the hardest strikers of the ball in the history of cricket. His sledgehammer shots struck the boundary before most fielders had a chance to react.

He was especially powerful off the back foot. As C.L.R. James wrote, 'We may some day be able to answer the... question: what is art? – but only when we learn to integrate our vision of Walcott on the back foot through the covers with the outstretched arm of the Olympic Apollo.'

He had a peerless off drive, and a dazzling square cut, and he was a superb hooker of the ball – according to James, on a par with Bradman.

Walcott accumulated 3,798 runs, including 15 centuries at an average of 56.68 in 44 Tests. His highest score was 220. As a wicketkeeper he took 27 catches and made 11 stumpings in 15 Tests. He was also a reasonable medium pace bowler.

Walcott was *Wisden* Cricketer of the Year in 1958.

After he retired Walcott went to live in Guyana where he groomed a galaxy of cricketing stars, including Kanhai, Butcher, Solomon, Gibbs and Lloyd. Walcott has received many honours including the OBE and a knighthood in 1994. Sir Clyde served as manager on various West Indies tours, and later as President of the West Indian Board. He was also President of the International Cricket Council and an ICC Test Match referee.

Gifted from an early age, Walcott started playing for his school at 12. At the age of 19 while playing for Barbados against Trinidad he scored 314 not out (his highest first-class score) in a record unbroken partnership with Worrell.

He made his Test debut in 1948 against the touring England team in the first Test in Barbados. This was the first series in which the three 'W's played together.

But it was on the 1948-49 tour of India that Walcott announced his arrival on the international scene with a flourish. He top scored with 152 in the first Test at Delhi; made 68 in the second Test in Bombay; and hit another century (108) in the third Test at Calcutta. He amassed 452 runs at an average of 65.57.

On the West Indies' historic tour of England in 1950, it was his 168 not out in the second Test at Lord's which contributed most to the West Indies' first Test victory over England in England. His prowess behind the stumps was also invaluable for Ramadhin and Valentine on that tour. He scored 1,674 first-class runs on the tour, including seven centuries, at an average of 55.80.

Walcott started playing for Enfield in the Lancashire League from 1951.

Walcott had a successful series against India in the Caribbean in 1953-54. In the second Test in Barbados he made 98. He later scored his first Test century in the Caribbean when he hit 125 in the fourth game in Guyana, and ended the series with 118 in Jamaica. His average was 76.16.

The next couple of years would see Walcott in devastating form. He had a superb series against England in the Caribbean in 1953-54. He scored 65 in the first Test in Jamaica; a double century (220, his highest Test score) in the second match in Barbados - regarded as his finest Test innings and one of the finest by a West Indian; 124 and 51 not out in the fourth Test in Trinidad; and 50 and 116 in the final match in Jamaica - ending the series with 698 runs for an astounding average of 87.25.

In 1954-55 it was the Australians - and Lindwall and Miller in particular - who had to bear the brunt of the assault of someone who most acknowledged to be the best batsman in the world at the time. Walcott scored five centuries in three Tests against the best bowling attack in the world.

In the first Test in Jamaica, he scored 108 (he also took 3 for 50, his best bowling figures). In the second game in Trinidad he scored 126 and 110. In the third Test in Guyana, he scored 73, and made 83 in the fourth Test in Barbados. And in the final Test in Jamaica, he scored 155 and 110. He ended the series with an aggregate of 827 - the highest in a series in the Caribbean - and an average of 82.70. Moreover, he was the first batsman to score a century in each innings twice in a Test series.

Against Pakistan in the Caribbean in 1957-58, Walcott scored 385 runs at an average of 96.25, including 145 in the fourth Test in Guyana.

After the English tour of the Caribbean in 1959-60, Walcott retired from international cricket.

CAREER STATISTICS

Sir Clyde Leopold Walcott • Barbados • 1952 • Right-hand batsman • Right-arm medium pace bowler
Test debut: v. England at Bridgetown, 1948

TESTS

Batting & Fielding	M	I	NO	Runs	HS	Ave	100	50	Ct	St
	44	74	7	3798	220	56.68	15	14	53	11

Bowling	O	M	R	W	Ave	BBI	5	10	SR	Econ
	199	72	408	11	37.09	3-50	0	0	108.5	2.05

FIRST-CLASS (1941/42-1963/64)

Batting & Fielding	M	I	NO	Runs	HS	Ave	100	50	Ct	St
	146	238	29	11820	314*	56.55	40	54	174	33

Bowling	Balls	M	R	W	Ave	BBI	5	10	SR	Econ
	3449	184	1269	35	36.25	5-41	1	0	98.5	2.20

SIR
EVERTON DE COURCY WEEKES

BARBADOS

Sir Everton Weekes belongs in that pantheon of West Indian super batsmen that includes Challenor, Headley, Worrell, Walcott, Sobers, Richards and Lara.

Weekes was a classy stroke maker with superb technique and style, but also a batsman of explosive power and dazzling improvisation. Yet he only ever hit one six in Tests, and that by choice.
Weekes' reasoning was that you couldn't be caught if you hit it along the ground (many years later, Richards was to reason that you couldn't be caught if you hit it out of the ground).

It was Weekes more than any batsman who most often elicited the phrase 'not a man moved'. For example, he reached his first century in England in 1950 in the third Test at Old Trafford in three successive balls, with a square cut, a cover drive, and another square cut off Alec Bedser, and all racing past Washbrook at cover point so fast that they hit the boundary before he could turn to retrieve the ball.

Short, solidly built and quick-footed, he terrorised bowlers with ferocious cuts, hooks, and drives on both sides of the wicket. He was considered by many as the best batsman of the three 'W's. He was also a superb close fielder.

John Arlott had this to say of Weekes: 'I admired Frank Worrell immensely, but Everton Weekes was the most explosive cricketer of all. He had incredible speed of footwork and stroke making. He was like Bradman but more extravagant.'

Sir Everton amassed 4,455 Test runs, including 15 centuries, at an average of 58.61 in 48 Tests. His highest score was 207. He still holds the record for the most consecutive Test centuries (5). Weekes' Test average is second to that of Headley (60.83) among West Indies batsmen.

Weekes was *Wisden* Cricketer of the Year in 1951.

After retiring Weekes spent a lot of time coaching youngsters in Barbados. In 1968 he was appointed manager of the West Indies team for the England tour of the Caribbean. He also served on the West Indies Cricket Board and as an ICC match referee. He was for many years a knowledgeable cricket commentator on Barbadian radio. Weekes has received many honours including a knighthood in 1995 for his services to cricket.

CAREER HIGHLIGHTS

Weekes, along with Worrell and Walcott, made his entry into Test cricket in the first Test series against England after the war in 1947-48 in the Caribbean. He scored 141 in the fourth and final Test in Jamaica.

But it was not until the following tour of India in 1948-49, that Weekes established beyond any doubt his formidable reputation as a world-class batsman. He had a magnificent series. He hit 128 in the first Test at Delhi, a superb 194 in the second Test at Bombay, 162 and 101 in the two innings of the third Test at Calcutta, and was controversially run out on 90 in the fourth Test at Madras. He scored an aggregate of 779 runs at an average of 111.28 for the series, and set a record of five consecutive Test centuries.

On the historic 1950 tour of England, Weekes scored 2,310 first-class runs at an average of 79.65. In the Tests he scored 338 runs at an average of 56.33, with 129 in the third Test at Trent Bridge. The three 'W's, along with Ramadhin and Valentine, led the West Indies to a triumphant 3-1 victory over England in England for the first time.

Facing India once again in 1952-53, this time in the Caribbean, Weekes was at his scintillating best. He hit 207 in the first Test in Trinidad; 161 and 55 not out in the third Test also in Trinidad; 86 in the fourth Test in Guyana; and 109 in the final Test in Jamaica (in that same match Worrell made 237 and Walcott 118!). Weekes headed the batting for the series with 716 runs at an average of 102.28.

Against England in the Caribbean in 1953-54 Weekes hit 55 and 90 not out in the first Test in Jamaica, 94 in the third Test in Guyana, and a magnificent 206 in the fourth Test in Trinidad (including a partnership of 338 with Frank Worrell).

Against Australia in the Caribbean in 1954-55, Weekes and Walcott savaged the bowling. Between them they scored 9 centuries and numerous fifties. In the second Test in Trinidad, Weekes scored 139 (the innings with the only six in his Test career) and 87 not out. He hit 81 in the third Test and 44 and 56 in the last two Tests. Despite this, however, Australia won the series 3-0.

On the 1955-56 tour of New Zealand, Weekes scored five centuries in the first five games. He hit 940 first-class runs at an average of 104.44. In the three Tests he hit 123 at Dunedin, 103 at Christ Church, and 156 at Wellington.

Against Pakistan in the Caribbean in 1957-58, Weekes hit 197 in the first Test in Barbados, and scored fifties in the two Tests in Trinidad. He finished this, his last series, with 455 runs at an average of 65.

He retired at the early age of 33.

Weekes also played for Bacup in the Lancashire League for six years from 1949 scoring 8,036 runs for an average of 91.32

Sir Everton de Courcy Weekes • Barbados • 1925 • Right-hand batsman • Right-arm leg-break bowler
Test debut: v. England at Bridgetown, 1948

TESTS

Batting & Fielding	M	I	NO	Runs	HS	Ave	100	50	Ct	St
	48	81	5	4455	207	58.61	15	19	49	0

Bowling	O	M	R	W	Ave	BBI	5	10	SR	Econ
	20.2	3	77	1	77.00	1-8	0	0	122.0	3.78

FIRST-CLASS (1944/45-1963/64)

Batting & Fielding	M	I	NO	Runs	HS	Ave	100	50	Ct	St
	152	241	24	12010	304*	55.34	36	54	125	1

Bowling	Balls	M	R	W	Ave	BBI	5	10	SR	Econ
	1125	18	731	17	43.00	4-38	0	0	66.1	3.89

SIR
FRANK MORTIMER WORRELL

BARBADOS

A genius of a batsman, Frank Worrell was also the first black series captain of the West Indies and one of the all-time great captains in cricket. So much so that his captaincy often overshadows what was a brilliant batting career. He was one of the best of his era, and one of the great three 'W's who dominated West Indian and world cricket in the 1950s.

As a captain Worrell was a great leader. He was calm, soft-spoken but firm, and imbued the team with a sense of professionalism and discipline. He was also a great student of the game and an original thinker. He had the additional advantage of being older than the rest of his team, which created affection and respect among the men he led. But he could also lead by example with both bat and ball.

Worrell, like Constantine, had an acute awareness of the prevailing injustices of the social order of his time. He was also a man of genuine Caribbean sensibility (born in Barbados, he also lived in Jamaica and Trinidad) who intensely disliked the insularity that has been the bane of the West Indies, in cricket as in so many other things.

The half a million people who lined the streets of Melbourne in 1961 to say farewell to the West Indies team were paying a tribute not only to the enterprising and entertaining cricket Worrell's team had played, but also to the dignity, decency and charm of the man. He was a graceful and stylish batsman, blessed with touch and elegance. He had near perfect balance and timing and nimble footwork, with a classically sound technique (he rarely played across the line) and an array of exquisite strokes. He was master of the delicate late cut. Neville Cardus wrote of Worrell that he never made a crude or ungrammatical stroke. He was an artist with the bat.

In 51 Tests he scored 3,860 runs, including nine centuries, at an average of 49.49. His highest Test score was 261, considered one of the greatest innings by a West Indian batsman.

He bowled left slow and medium, and like Sobers after him, started his first-class career as a bowler who could also bat. He was an effective bowler who took 69 Test wickets at an average of 38.72. His best figures were 7 for 70.

As captain of the West Indies he won 9 lost 3 drew 2 and tied 1.

Worrell was *Wisden* Cricketer of the Year in 1951.

As Worrell noted on his retirement, 'My aim was always to see West Indies moulded from a rabble of brilliant island individualists into a real team - and I've done it.' How many a Caribbean statesmen might have wished to say the same thing about the West Indian integration movement!

Worrell was knighted in 1964 for his services to the game. He was also appointed Warden of a hall of residence at the University of the West Indies, and became a senator in the Jamaican Parliament.

In 1967 he died of leukaemia at the age of 43. Flags flew at half mast in Barbados, Jamaica and Radcliffe, England, and a memorial service was held at Westminster Abbey, the first time such an honour had been accorded to a cricketer.

Sir Frank was buried at the Cave Hill campus of UWI in Barbados where the cricket ground is named after the three 'W's.

CAREER HIGHLIGHTS

A teenage cricketing prodigy, Frank Worrell, like Sir Everton Weekes, played for the famous Empire Club after he left school. The house where he lived still stands just outside the cricket ground.

Worrell, along with Walcott and Weekes, made his debut for the West Indies against England in the Caribbean in the first post-war Test series in 1947-48. He made 97 in his first Test innings in the second Test in Trinidad. In the third Test in Guyana, he made a glorious 131 not out, and in the final Test in Jamaica a stylish 38 to end the series with 294 at an average of 147.00.

On the West Indies' tour of England in 1950 Worrell performed brilliantly. He scored 52 and 45 in the second Test at Lord's, and then a magnificent 261 in the third Test at Trent Bridge. This was ranked by *Wisden* as one of the great Test innings of all time. Worrell scored 138 in the fourth and final Test at The Oval. He finished the series as the leading batsman with 539 runs at an average of 89.93.

On the disappointing tour of Australia in 1951-52, Worrell, like the other West Indies batsmen, found it difficult to cope with the Australian pace attack. Nevertheless in the fourth Test at Melbourne he took the attack to Lindwall and Miller and scored a brilliant 108. He ended the series as the leading batsman with 337 runs at 33.70 and took 19 wickets at 21.57, including 6 for 38 in the third Test at Adelaide.

Against India in the Caribbean in 1952-53, Worrell scored a glorious 237 in the fifth Test in Jamaica.

When England toured the Caribbean in 1953-54 Worrell was appointed vice-captain. He scored a masterful 167 and 56 in the fourth Test in Trinidad.

On the disastrous (0-3) tour of England in 1957, Worrell led the first-class averages with 1,470 runs at an average of 58.80 and took 39 wickets at 24.33. He began with 81 in the first Test at Edgbaston; 191 in the third Test at Trent Bridge (opening the batting); and took 7 for 70 in the fourth Test at Headingley (opening the bowling with Gilchrist).

Worrell withdrew from cricket for a couple of years to complete his studies at Manchester University. When he returned, the second part of his career turned out to be even more brilliant. On the England tour of the Caribbean in 1959-60, Worrell made 197 not out, lasting 11 hours and 29 minutes, including a partnership of 399 with Garry Sobers, in the first Test in Barbados. He took 4 for 49 in the fourth Test in Guyana, and finished the series with 61 in the fifth Test in Trinidad.

These performances, coupled with a public campaign led by C.L.R. James, forced the West Indies Cricket Board of Control to concede what the public in the West Indies had known for a long time: that Worrell was the natural choice for captain of the West Indies team.

Worrell instilled a high degree of professionalism in his team, enjoyed the confidence and affection of his men, and was an extraordinary leader on and off the field. On his first tour as captain - the historic tour to Australia - Worrell lost the series by the narrowest of margins, but his attacking and attractive style of cricket won the heart of the Australian cricket public.

That tour also had a significance beyond the boundary. It put paid to the notorious 'white only' captaincy of the West Indies that had been the bane of our cricket, and it sent a positive message to Australians, who at the time had a 'white only' immigration policy.

The revitalised West Indies team thrashed the Indians 5-0 when they toured the Caribbean in 1961-62. Worrell headed the batting averages with 88.00.

On the 1963 tour of England, Worrell led his team to victory by a margin of 3-1. The series was a thrilling one, with *Wisden* declaring that 'no more popular side have ever toured the old country.'

Worrell retired at the age of 39. One of his great cricketing opponents, Richie Benaud of Australia, said of Sir Frank: 'There is no doubt in my mind that he is the most important cricketer ever to play the game in the Caribbean as well as one of the finest men ever to grace the game.'

CAREER STATISTICS

Sir Frank Mortimer Maglinne Worrell • Barbados • 1924-1967 • Right-hand batsman • Left-arm slow and medium pace bowler
Test debut: v. England at Port-of-Spain, 1948

TESTS

Batting & Fielding	M	I	NO	Runs	HS	Ave	100	50	Ct	St
	51	87	9	3860	261	49.48	9	22	43	0

Bowling	Balls	M	R	W	Ave	BBI	5	10	SR	Econ
	7141	274	2672	69	38.72	7-70	2	0	103.4	2.24

FIRST-CLASS (1941/42-1963/64)

Batting & Fielding	M	I	NO	Runs	HS	Ave	100	50	Ct	St
	208	326	49	15025	308*	54.24	39	80	139	0

Bowling	Balls	M	R	W	Ave	BBI	5	10	SR	Econ
	26740	1123	10115	349	28.98	7-70	13	0	76.6	2.26

THE WORRELL-S

OBERS ERA

1960-74

THIS PERIOD BEGAN UNDER THE CAPTAINCY OF WORRELL, WHO

MOULDED A BAND OF BRILLIANT INDIVIDUALS INTO A WORLD-

BEATING TEAM. SOBERS SUCCEEDED WORRELL AND CARRIED

FORWARD HIS WINNING WAYS. BUT TOWARDS THE END OF THE

PERIOD THE WEST INDIES BEGAN TO FALTER. THE GREATS OF

THIS ERA ARE GIBBS, HALL, HUNTE, KANHAI AND SOBERS.

LANCELOT RICHARD GIBBS

GUYANA

Lance Gibbs is without doubt the best West Indies spin bowler, and one of the finest off-spin bowlers the world has ever seen. He was the first spin bowler to pass 300 Test wickets.

For a spinner to maintain a place in the West Indies team he had to be remarkably good to break the stranglehold fast bowlers had. Gibbs, for a while, even overshadowed them. Curiously enough, Gibbs started as a leg-spinner, but switched fairly early on in his first-class career.

He had an unorthodox chest-on action, and delivered the ball from a great height and with his long fingers was able to extract the maximum spin and bounce. He was a master at varying pace and flight, and was renowned for his incredible accuracy and control.

The statistics bear out Gibbs' claim to fame: in 79 Tests he earned 309 wickets at an average of 29.09. He was the first West Indies bowler to take 300 wickets. He took five or more wickets in a Test innings no fewer than eighteen times. He also had the distinction of taking a Test hat trick, against Australia on the famous 1960-61 tour. He had the amazing figures in a Test match of 53.3 overs, 37 maidens, 8 for 39 against India at Kensington Oval in Barbados in 1962. He was also an excellent close fielder, especially at gully.

Gibbs was *Wisden* Cricketer of the Year in 1972.

After retiring, Gibbs moved to the United States and worked in shipping. But he was not entirely lost to West Indies cricket and managed the team in 1990. He has also been involved in coaching young West Indies players.

CAREER HIGHLIGHTS

Gibbs made his Test debut against Pakistan in the West Indies in 1958. He had a great series, heading the bowling averages with 17 wickets at an average of 23.05, including 5 for 80 in the fourth Test in Guyana.

Gibbs really came into his own on the West Indies' tour of Australia in 1960-61. He was not picked for the first two Tests, but in the third Test, replacing Ramadhin, he took 3 wickets in 4 balls, propelling the West Indies to victory. In the fourth Test he took a hat trick, dismissing Mackay, Grout and Misson in successive balls. He followed this up with 4 for 74 in the final Test and was, after playing in only three Tests, the leading West Indies wicket-taker.

Against India in the Caribbean in 1962, Gibbs, in one magnificent spell of fine spin bowling, took 8 wickets for 6 runs in 15.3 overs including 14 maidens, to help the West Indies to an incredible victory in the third Test in Barbados. He finished with figures of 8 for 39.

For more than a decade after this, Gibbs was recognised as the finest off-spinner in the world and held his place in the West Indies team despite the emphasis on pace. On the 1963 tour of England, Gibbs took 9 for 157 in the first Test. He ended up with figures of 26 wickets at an average of 21.30.

Against Australia in the Caribbean in 1964-65, Gibbs outperformed Hall and Griffith. He took 3 for 51 and 6 for 29 in the third Test in Guyana, and finished as the leading wicket-taker for the West Indies with 18. He was instrumental in the West Indies winning their first ever series victory over Australia.

In the 1966 series against England, he topped the bowling averages again, and took 10 wickets in the first Test, as well as 6 for 39 in the second innings of the fourth Test.

In 1969 Gibbs took a break from cricket until 1972, when he played again for the West Indies against Australia in the Caribbean, picking up 26 wickets at an average of 26.76 in the five matches. This was followed by a magnificent tour of India in 1974-75 when he took 6 for 76 and 7 for 98 in the second and fifth Tests.

It was during the 1975-76 tour of Australia that Gibbs became the leading wicket-taker in the world with 309 wickets. Gibbs retired after this series at the age of 42.

Gibbs also played first-class cricket in the Lancashire and Durham Leagues and for Warwickshire.

CAREER STATISTICS

Lancelot Richard Gibbs • Guyana • 1934 • Right-arm off-spin bowler • Right-hand batsman
Test debut: v. Pakistan at Port-of-Spain, 1958

TESTS

Batting & Fielding	M	I	NO	Runs	HS	Ave	100	50	Ct	St
	79	109	39	488	25	6.97	0	0	52	0

Bowling	Balls	M	R	W	Ave	BBI	5	10	SR	Econ
	27155	1313	8989	309	29.09	8-38	18	2	87.7	1.98

FIRST-CLASS (1953/54-1974/75)

Batting & Fielding	M	I	NO	Runs	HS	Ave	100	50	Ct	St
	330	352	150	1729	43	8.55	0	0	203	0

Bowling	Balls	M	R	W	Ave	BBI	5	10	SR	Econ
	78430	3757	27878	1024	27.22	8-37	50	10	76.5	2.13

WESLEY WINFIELD HALL

BARBADOS

Wes Hall formed, with fellow Barbadian Charlie Griffith, one of the famous and feared West Indian opening pace attacks. During the 1960s they blazed the trail for the succession of lethal fast bowlers who made the West Indies the best and most feared team from the mid-seventies to the early nineties.

Well over six feet and broad-shouldered, Hall had a smooth and classic action off a famously long run. He was genuinely quick ('pace like fire' to use the title of his autobiography), and swung the ball effectively. The sight of Hall running up to bowl with gold chain flapping against his chest terrorised many a batsman.
His bouncers were notorious. He was one of the finest fast bowlers in the world.

Hall was also blessed with great stamina, often bowling for well over an hour in a spell. He was the first West Indian bowler to take a hat trick in a Test match - against Pakistan at Lahore in 1958-59. He also bowled the last over in the famous tied Test with Australia at Brisbane in 1960.

Hall played in 48 Tests, taking 192 wickets at an average of 26.38. A stand at Kensington Oval was erected to honour the outstanding contribution of Wes Hall and Charlie Griffith.

After he retired, Hall entered politics as a senator and subsequently an elected member of the House of Assembly and Minister of Tourism and Sport in Barbados. Hall has remained actively involved in cricket as a manager of the West Indies team (1993-96), a chairman of selectors and most recently, as the President of the West Indies Cricket Board from July 2001 to July 2003.

CAREER HIGHLIGHTS

Wes Hall was included only as a last-minute replacement in the West Indies team to tour India and Pakistan in 1958-59. But he made his Test debut in impressive style. In the second Test against India at Kanpur, Hall had figures of 6-50 and 5-76. He ended up with 30 wickets at an average of 17.66.

In Pakistan, he took 4-28 and 4-49 in the two innings of the second Test at Dacca. In the third and final Test at Lahore, Hall took the only hat trick of his career and finished with figures of 5 for 87. For the two series he took 46 wickets at an average of 17.76 in eight Tests.

Hall played a key role in the famous tied Test in the opening game of the Australian tour at Brisbane in 1960. He was asked by captain Worrell to bowl the last (8 ball) over, with Australia needing 6 runs to win. Hall had Benaud caught behind off the second ball. On the fifth ball Grout skied a catch to square leg which the bowler ought to have left to the fielder Kanhai. The catch was dropped and Australia scored two more runs. Ian Meckiff hit the sixth ball to backward square leg and attempting a third run was run out by a brilliant throw from Hunte, with the scores tied. The last Australian to bat, Kline, received a blistering delivery from Hall, got his bat on it and attempted a run. Solomon ran out Meckiff and so created the first tied Test in history.

Hall's good showing on the tour led to an invitation to play for Queensland.

On the 1962 India tour of the Caribbean, Hall excelled with 27 wickets at an average of 15.74. In the second Test in Jamaica, he took 5 for 49 in the second innings to lead West Indies to victory. In the fourth Test in Trinidad, he took 5 for 20.

On the West Indies' tour of England in 1963, Hall, in an impressive display of stamina, bowled unchanged for three hours and twenty minutes in the second Test at Lord's, taking 4 for 93 from 40 overs in the second innings. He also took 4 for 39 in the second innings of the fifth Test at The Oval.

On the 1964-65 Australian tour of the Caribbean, Hall took 5 for 60 and 4 for 45 in the first Test in Jamaica, giving the West Indies their first victory over Australia in the Caribbean.

After the 1968-69 tour of Australia and New Zealand Hall retired from Test cricket.

Wesley Winfield Hall • Barbados • 1937 • Right-arm fast bowler • Right-hand batsman
Test debut: v. India at Bombay, 1958-59

TESTS

Batting & Fielding	M	I	NO	Runs	HS	Ave	100	50	Ct	St
	48	66	14	818	50*	15.73	0	2	11	0

Bowling	Balls	M	R	W	Ave	BBI	5	10	SR	Econ
	10421	312	5066	192	26.38	7-69	9	1	54.2	2.91

FIRST-CLASS (1955/56-1970/71)

Batting & Fielding	M	I	NO	Runs	HS	Ave	100	50	Ct	St
	170	215	38	2673	102*	15.10	1	6	58	0

Bowling	Balls	M	R	W	Ave	BBI	5	10	SR	Econ
	25082	801	14273	546	26.14	7-51	19	2	51.4	3.04

SIR
CONRAD CLEOPHAS HUNTE

BARBADOS

Conrad Hunte was one of the best opening batsmen the West Indies ever produced. He was certainly the first dominant opening batsman for the West Indies and the role model for Greenidge and Haynes.

Unlike Greenidge and Haynes, however, Hunte never had a steady opening partner. He opened with twelve different partners in his 44 Tests, which undoubtedly put a lot of pressure on him. Contrast this with the 89 Tests that Greenidge and Haynes played together.

Hunte was a natural and fluent strokemaker who drove beautifully off the front foot, although he tended to favour the back foot. He was master of the cut, but could hook and pull with the best of them. At the same time, Hunte had a technically solid defence and he often played with great restraint, especially in his later years.

Hunte was one of the shining lights of the West Indies teams of the 1960s. His presence at the top of the order and his role as vice-captain to Worrell was instrumental in the rise of the West Indies to the top of the cricketing world under Worrell and later Sobers.

Hunte scored 3,245 Test runs including eight centuries and thirteen fifties, at an average of 45.06. His highest Test score was 260 against Pakistan in Jamaica in 1958.

Hunte was *Wisden* Cricketer of the Year in 1964.

After retirement, at the invitation of the South Africa Cricket Board, Hunte spent seven years teaching cricket in the townships and helping the youth to a better life. As his good friend Ali Bacher said at his funeral, 'Today thousands and thousands of young South Africans are better because of his influence. We regard him as one of our greatest adopted sons.'

While in South Africa Hunte served as the Honorary Consul of Barbados in the late 1990s. He was knighted in 1998. Hunte was elected President of the Barbados Cricket Association in 1999, but a few weeks later died of a heart attack at the age of 67 while visiting Sydney, where he had gone to make a keynote speech at a Moral Rearmament conference.

Sir Conrad was given an official funeral, which was televised from Barbados across the Caribbean.

Conrad Hunte had a belated but dazzling introduction to Test cricket in 1958 against Pakistan in Barbados. He scored 142. In the third Test in Jamaica, he scored 260 and featured in a record second-wicket partnership of 446 with Garry Sobers. Hunte capped the series with another hundred in the fourth Test in Guyana, ending with an aggregate of 662 and an average of 75.55. Quite a debut!

Hunte had a great tour of Australia in 1960, with sound performances including 110 in the second innings of the second Test in Melbourne.

In the 1963 tour of England Hunte had a superb series. He scored 471 Test runs and topped the averages with 58.87. In the first Test at Old Trafford he made 182 in 8 hours to help the West Indies to victory. In the fifth Test at The Oval he made 80 and 108, again contributing to a West Indies victory in the match, and the series 3-1.

Hunte served as vice-captain to Worrell in 1963 and was widely expected to be appointed captain on Worrell's retirement. Garry Sobers, however, was made captain much to Hunte's disappointment. It was felt that Hunte's intense commitment to Moral Rearmament might have interfered with his responsibilities as captain.

In the 1964-65 series against Australia in the Caribbean he topped the averages again, hitting five half centuries and scoring 550 runs at an average of 61.11.

Hunte had a good tour of India in 1966-67. In the three-match series he scored a century in the first Test at Bombay and got past 40 in his next three innings.

Hunte retired from the game after that tour.

CAREER STATISTICS

Sir Conrad Cleophas Hunte • Barbados • 1932-1999 • Right-hand opening batsman • Right-arm medium pace bowler
Test debut: v. Pakistan at Bridgetown, 1958

TESTS

Batting & Fielding	M	I	NO	Runs	HS	Ave	100	50	Ct	St
	44	78	6	3245	260	45.06	8	13	16	0

Bowling	O	M	R	W	Ave	BBI	5	10	SR	Econ
	45	11	110	2	55.00	1-17	0	0	135.0	2.44

FIRST-CLASS (1950/51-1966/67)

Batting & Fielding	M	I	NO	Runs	HS	Ave	100	50	Ct	St
	132	222	19	8916	263	43.92	16	51	68	1

Bowling	Balls	M	R	W	Ave	BBI	5	10	SR	Econ
	-	-	644	17	37.88	3-5	0	0	-	-

ROHAN BHOLALLAL KANHAI

GUYANA

Kanhai was a brilliant and elegant attacking batsman, comfortable against pace or spin. A short man, 5'7", he combined extravagant stroke play with a sound defensive technique. He had great reflexes and timing and a dazzling variety of strokes. He could caress fast bowlers to the boundary with consummate ease.

But perhaps he is most famous for being a highly innovative and audacious batsman, known for his extravagant 'fall down' hook, in which, as the ball hit or soared over the boundary, Kanhai was lying on his back. C.L.R. James described him as 'adventuresome'. He also had the concentration that allowed him to play a long patient innings to save his team. He was a superb cover fielder.

In the early sixties he was part of a great West Indies middle order that included Sobers, Butcher, Nurse and Worrell.

Kanhai scored an aggregate of 6,277 runs, including 15 centuries and 28 half centuries, at an average of 47.53 in 79 Tests. He was *Wisden* Cricketer of the Year in 1964.

After retiring in 1974, he coached the Jamaican national team as well as West Indies teams at junior and senior level. Kanhai has a stand named after him at the Bourda cricket ground in Guyana.

CAREER HIGHLIGHTS

Kanhai made his Test debut on the West Indies' disastrous tour of England in 1957, when he kept wicket in the first three Tests, before Franz Alexander took over. He was also asked to open in the first two Tests but was then allowed to revert to his natural middle order position. During the series he made three 40s and top scored with 34 out of 127 in the first innings of the second Test at Lord's.

After a solid series at home against Pakistan in 1958, he scored a magnificent 256 - his first Test century - in the third Test at Calcutta on the tour of India and Pakistan in 1958-59. He accumulated 538 runs at an average of 67.25. On the Pakistan leg of the tour, he scored a superb 217 in the third Test at Lahore.

These performances sealed his place in the West Indies team. He was compared to Weekes with his sweeping and hooking. He soon established himself as a world-class batsman.

He really sparkled on the famous tour of Australia in 1960-61, amassing 1,083 first-class runs at an average of 64.29, and 503 Test runs at an average of 50.30. He began by scoring a century against an Australia XI and a double against Victoria. He hit 54 in the first Test at Brisbane; 84 in the second Test at Melbourne; and 117 and 115 in both innings of the fourth Test at Adelaide, at almost a run a minute.

This was followed by a good series against India in the Caribbean in 1961-62, with centuries in the second and fourth Tests, and an aggregate of 495 runs at an average of 70.71.

On the 1963 tour of England, although he did not score a century, Kanhai had a number of decisive innings: 90 in the first Test at Old Trafford; 73 in the second Test at Lord's; 92 in the fourth Test at Headingley and a sparkling 77 in the final Test at The Oval. He ended up with 497 runs at an average of 55.22.

On the 1964-65 Australian tour of the Caribbean, Kanhai scored centuries in the fourth Test in Barbados and in the fifth Test in Trinidad.

On the England tour of the Caribbean in 1968 Kanhai was in dazzling form, scoring 85 in the first Test in Trinidad, a superb 153 in the fourth Test also in Trinidad, and a century in the final Test in Guyana.

One of his greatest innings was 115 - largely off the bowling of Dennis Lillee - playing for the Rest of the World against Australia in 1971-72.

Kanhai was appointed captain against the touring Australians in 1972-73. Although the West Indies lost the series, he did well with the bat, hitting 84 in the first Test in Jamaica, top scoring with a century in the second Test in Barbados, and making half centuries in the Tests in Trinidad and Guyana.

He had better luck as captain against England on the West Indies tour later that year. The West Indies won the three-Test series, with Kanhai cracking 157 in the final Test at Lord's, the first series win since 1967. He ended the tour with an average of 50.20.

In his thirteen Tests as captain Kanhai instilled the killer instinct in the side which Lloyd was to build on during West Indies dominance of international cricket.

Kanhai retired in 1974 at the age of 39.

Kanhai also played for Western Australia in 1961 and later for Warwickshire scoring 1,000 first-class runs in each of his ten seasons with them.

CAREER STATISTICS

Rohan Bholallal Kanhai • Guyana • 1935 • Right-hand batsman • Right-arm medium pace bowler • Wicketkeeper
Test debut: v. England at Birmingham, 1957

TESTS

Batting & Fielding	M	I	NO	Runs	HS	Ave	100	50	Ct	St
	79	137	6	6227	256	47.53	15	28	50	0

Bowling	Balls	M	R	W	Ave	BBI	5	10	SR	Econ
	183	8	85	0	-	-	0	0	-	2.78

FIRST-CLASS (1954/55-1977)

Batting & Fielding	M	I	NO	Runs	HS	Ave	100	50	Ct	St
	416	669	82	28774	256	49.01	83	120	319	7

Bowling	Balls	M	R	W	Ave	BBI	5	10	SR	Econ
	1505	35	1009	18	56.05	2-5	0	0	83.6	4.02

THE RIGHT EXCELLENT
SIR GARFIELD
ST. AUBRUN SOBERS

BARBADOS

Garfield St. Aubrun Sobers is the greatest all-rounder in the history of cricket and one of the six best batsmen of all time. He was chosen as one of the five *Wisden* Cricketers of the Century in 2000 the others being Don Bradman, Jack Hobbs, Viv Richards and Shane Warne. Sobers, W.G. Grace and Don Bradman are the three indisputable superstars of cricket.

Sobers was a genius of a cricketer: a master batsman, a superb fast bowler and a spinner of all varieties. He was also one of the greatest fielders of all time. He was a naturally attacking batsman and played to perfection every shot in the book. Yet he could put together a careful, restrained innings on a sticky wicket in difficult circumstances for his team. His six-hour-long 113 not out on a nightmare of a pitch at Sabina Park in 1968 against England is one of the most extraordinary innings in cricket.

His batting was pure joy to watch, exemplifying sheer joie de vivre. He truly stood on the shoulders of Challenor, Headley, and especially the great three 'W's, combining Worrell's grace, Walcott's power and Weekes' dynamism with his own athletic suppleness to produce a style of batting that was uniquely his own.

He hit the ball with great power from a high backlift, but could also use his wrists to flick the ball effortlessly off his pads to the midwicket boundary. Tall and lithe,

he had a perfect technique, although he had received no formal coaching. He rarely hit across the line, played with a straight bat and had an amazing variety of strokes.

He was also one of those rare cricketers - Brian Lara is another - who never waited for an umpire's decision if he knew he had edged the ball and it had been caught. He would walk immediately. He was a sporting person to the core. A key ingredient in his success was his fierce competitiveness and his total commitment.

His captaincy of the West Indies was always a subject of debate. Some considered that he took unnecessary chances in the expectation that his team mates would perform with the bat and ball as he did. He certainly was an aggressive captain who played to win rather than draw. He was captain for 39 Tests of which he won nine and lost ten.

Sobers' figures speak volumes. For over three

decades he held the world record for the highest Test score of 365 not out against Pakistan in 1958. It was broken by Brian Lara in 1994 with his 375. Sobers amassed 8,032 runs, including 26 centuries at an average of 57.78 in 93 Tests, a West Indies total surpassed so far only by Viv Richards and Brian Lara, and an average surpassed only by Headley and Weekes. He took 235 Test wickets and held 109 catches. He was also the first batsman to hit six sixes in one over, in 1968 while playing for Nottinghamshire against Glamorgan.

Sobers was *Wisden* Cricketer of the Year in 1964. He was married to an Australian, Prue Kirby, and still regards Australia as a second home. In 1975, in an unprecedented open-air ceremony at the Garrison Savannah in Barbados, less than a mile from where he had grown up, Sobers was knighted by the Queen before thousands of his adoring fans for his outstanding contribution to cricket.

CAREER PROFILE

Sir Garfield has received numerous honours and accolades. He is a recipient of Trinidad and Tobago's highest honour, The Trinity Cross, as well as the Order of the Caribbean Community. In 1998 Barbados declared him a National Hero. A statue was erected in his honour in Barbados in 2002.

He was awarded the Australian Order in 2003.

Sir Garfield currently serves as a sports consultant with the Barbados Tourism Authority. He also founded the Sir Garfield Sobers International Schoolboys Tournament,

held in Barbados annually. When one thinks of Sir Garry's achievements, one cannot help recalling the statement made by Tostao on the 60th birthday of his Brazilian team mate Pele: 'Idols and myths grow old and die but their works of art are eternal.'

CAREER HIGHLIGHTS

Sobers began his Test career in 1954 at the age of 17, playing against England in the final Test in Jamaica as a spin bowler, taking 4 for 75. Four years later, in the fourth Test against Pakistan, at the ripe old age of 21, Sobers made his first Test century by beating Len Hutton's twenty-year-old record of the highest score in a Test (364) in a historic innings of 365 not out. It included 34 fours.

Sobers truly came of age and won international recognition in this series. After his triple in Jamaica, he made two single centuries in the fourth Test in Guyana, finishing the series with 824 runs at an average of 137.33!

For the next decade Sobers dominated international cricket at every level of the game. He followed up with a glorious tour of India in 1958-59, scoring 142

not out, 198, and 106 not out in the first three Tests. He amassed 557 runs at an average of 92.83. He also finished third in the bowling averages.

Back home in the Caribbean for the 1959-60 England tour, Sobers made a stylish 226 in the first Test in Barbados; 147 in the third Test in Jamaica; 145 in the fourth Test in Guyana; and 92 in the fifth Test in Trinidad. He finished the series with 709 runs at an average of 101.28.

On the famous West Indies tour of Australia in 1960-61, Sobers cemented his claim to be the best all-rounder in the world. It was on this tour that he first started to bowl medium fast, opening the bowling with Wes Hall. In the first and famous tied Test at Brisbane, Sobers scored 132 in a stylish and masterful knock that lasted 174 minutes and was one of the most beautiful displays of his career. It prompted Don Bradman to visit the dressing room to congratulate him, and was also described by Johnny Moyes as the most outstanding seen in Australia since the days of Bradman and McCabe.

In the third Test Sobers hit a brilliant 168 with a six and twenty-four fours. In the final Test at Melbourne he top scored with 64 in the West Indies' first innings and then took 5 for 120. He was invited to play for South Australia in the Sheffield Shield.

Sobers had a great series with the ball against India in the Caribbean in 1961-62 when he took 23 wickets at an average of 20.56. In the fifth Test in Jamaica Sobers scored a century and took five wickets in the second innings.

In 1965 Sobers was appointed captain for the home series against Australia, a post he went on to hold for 39 of his 93 Tests. Although he had a modest series with the bat, he led the West Indies to their first series victory (2-1) over Australia. He also took his 100th Test wicket during this series.

Sobers enjoyed a highly successful tour of England in 1966, leading the West Indies to a 3-1 victory. He scored 722 runs in the five Tests at an average of 103.14; took 20 wickets at an average of 27.25; and took 10 catches. He also passed 5,000 Test runs on this tour. He top scored with 161 in the first Test at

Old Trafford. He reached his century by hitting the English fast bowler John Snow for six over long-off, leading Colin Milburn to remark that he was ruining the game. In the second Test at Lord's Sobers completed one of his most memorable innings. Coming together with his cousin David Holford when the score was 95 for 5, Sobers went on to score 163 not out in an epic partnership of 274 with Holford (105) to save the match.

In the third Test at Trent Bridge he made a rapid 94 to set up a declaration and a West Indies win. In the fourth Test at Headingley he hit 174 (his highest Test score in England) and had match figures of 8 for 80 including 5 for 41 in England's second innings. In the fifth Test at The Oval, he scored 81 in the first innings in a losing cause.

When England toured the Caribbean in 1968, Sobers had a great series with the bat, scoring an extraordinary 113 on a horrible pitch in the second Test in Jamaica, and 152 and 95 not out in the fifth Test in Guyana, to end up with 545 runs at an average of 90.83. He also passed 6,000 runs. But the West Indies lost the series 1-0 after Sobers made a sporting declaration in the fourth Test in Trinidad and England won.

Sobers had his best Test bowling figures in the first Test at Brisbane against Australia in 1968: 6 for 73.

Away from the international circuit, Sobers was performing remarkably well in Australia and England. He became the first man to score 1,000 runs and take 50 wickets in one Australian season.

In England in 1968 he led Nottinghamshire from fifteenth to fourth in the County championship. Sobers topped the batting averages, was second in the bowling and took more catches than anyone else apart from the wicketkeeper. In that same year he wrote himself yet again into the record books and the public imagination when he hit six sixes in one over off Glamorgan's Malcolm Nash.

Sobers played what was probably the greatest innings of his life, at the age of 35, for the Rest of the World vs. Australia in the 1971-72 series in Australia. His 254 (6 sixes, 35 fours) at Melbourne was rated as even better than the brilliant 132 at Brisbane in the famous tied Test of 1960. Moreover, this was an innings played against the feared Dennis Lillee at his scorching best, and after he had dismissed Sobers for a duck in the first innings.

Sir Donald Bradman commented, 'The innings was probably the best ever played in Australia. The people who saw Sobers have enjoyed one of the historic events of cricket.' And *Wisden* observed, 'It was an unforgettable display, combining such elegance of stroke play, power and aggression that the crowds responded ecstatically.'

Sobers had his last great series with the bat against India in the Caribbean in 1970-71. In the first Test in Jamaica he scored 44 and 93; in the third Test in Guyana he scored 108 not out; in the fourth Test in Barbados he made 178 not out; and in the fifth Test in Trinidad he made 132; amassing 597 runs at an average of 74.62. This series also saw Sobers pass 7,000 runs and 200 wickets.

Sobers ended his Test appearances in England on a high note during the 1973 tour, under the captaincy of Kanhai, when, in the third Test at Lord's, he scored an unbeaten 150 (the last of his 26 Test centuries) and took a record six catches close to the wicket.

After the England tour of the West Indies in 1974, during which he became the first man to score 8,000 runs in Test cricket, Sobers retired from the game.

CAREER STATISTICS

Right Excellent Sir Garfield St. Aubrun Sobers • Barbados • 1936 • Left-hand batsman
Left-arm fast medium bowler • slow left-arm orthodox spinner • slow left-arm chinaman and googly bowler
Test debut: v. England at Kingston, 1954

TESTS

Batting & Fielding	M	I	NO	Runs	HS	Ave	100	50	Ct	St
	93	160	21	8032	365*	57.78	26	30	109	0

Bowling	Balls	M	R	W	Ave	BBI	5	10	SR	Econ
	21599	974	7999	235	34.03	6-73	6	0	91.9	2.22

FIRST-CLASS (1952/53-1974)

Batting & Fielding	M	I	NO	Runs	HS	Ave	100	50	Ct	St
	383	609	93	28314	365*	54.87	86	121	407	0

Bowling	Balls	M	R	W	Ave	BBI	5	10	SR	Econ
	70789	2890	28941	1043	27.74	9-49	36	1	67.8	2.45

WORLD SU

UPREMACY

1975-95

CLIVE LLOYD IN 1975 INSTITUTED THE FAMOUS FOUR-PRONGED
PACE ATTACK BACKED UP BY GREAT BATTING, AND THE REST IS
HISTORY. NO TEAM HAS EVER DOMINATED WORLD CRICKET AS
THE WEST INDIES DID DURING THIS PERIOD. THEY LOST ONLY
TWO OF THE THIRTY-FIVE SERIES THEY PLAYED DURING THESE
YEARS, AND THEY ENJOYED TWENTY-NINE CONSECUTIVE SERIES
WITHOUT A LOSS. IT IS THEREFORE NOT SURPRISING THAT
TWELVE OF THE TWENTY-FIVE GREATS ARE CHOSEN FROM THIS
ERA, SIX FAST BOWLERS AND SIX BATSMEN: AMBROSE, DUJON,
GARNER, GREENIDGE, HAYNES, HOLDING, KALLICHARRAN,
LLOYD, MARSHALL, RICHARDS, ROBERTS AND WALSH.

CURTLY ELCONN LYNWALL AMBROSE

ANTIGUA

Curtly Ambrose was one of the great West Indian fast bowlers. His height (6' 7") and suppleness of wrist allowed him to bounce the ball steeply off a good length. In his younger days he would intimidate with bouncers and yorkers. Never a great swinger of the ball, it was his nagging accuracy that was the basis of his phenomenal success.

When he lost some of his pace in his later years, bowling only medium-fast, his immaculate line and length and variation of speed made him a highly respected bowler. Even on those occasions when he did not take many wickets, his economy rate was so good that he kept unrelenting pressure on the batsmen.

Ambrose and Courtney Walsh were the last pair of first-class, consistently good, pace bowlers in the West Indies teams of the Lloyd and Richards era. They were one of the most successful fast bowling partnerships in the history of the game, taking 421 wickets between them in 49 Tests.

Curtly always maintained his fitness and had great stamina. He had a lot of heart and always gave it his all, even on the flattest of pitches.

He seemed to perform best against the English. In 34 Tests against England, he took an incredible 164 wickets. Ambrose took 405 wickets in 98 Tests at an average of 20.99 runs. He had five or more wickets in 22 innings. On three occasions he took 25 or more wickets in a series.

Ambrose was *Wisden* Cricketer of the Year in 1992.

Ambrose made his Test debut in the 1987-88 home series against Pakistan. But it was not until the 1988-89 tour of Australia that he established himself as one of the world's top fast bowlers. Australia had hoped that with the retirement of Roberts, Garner and Holding and the reduced speed of Marshall, they would get some relief from the unrelenting pace. But Ambrose combined with Walsh, Patterson and Marshall to produce spectacular performances to win the series for the West Indies by 3-1. Ambrose took 26 wickets at an average of 21.46.

Ambrose had a fine performance against England in the Caribbean in 1989-90. He had figures of 4 for 59, and a phenomenal 8 for 45, his best performance. He finished with 20 wickets at an average of 15.35.

Against Pakistan in 1990-91, Ambrose's best figures were 5 for 35 in the third Test. In 1991 against England, Ambrose had a fantastic series. He took 6 for 52 in the first Test and 5 for 74 in the third, finishing with 28 wickets at an average of 20.00.

In the one-off Test against South Africa at Bridgetown in 1992, Ambrose saved the day for the West Indies by capturing 6 for 34 in the second innings. This was one of his finest moments.

In a great series against Australia in 1992-93, Ambrose had hauls of 5 for 66 in the first Test, and 6 for 74 and 4 for 46 in both innings of the fourth Test, and, in a magnificent performance in the fifth Test, took 7 for 25, with all seven wickets coming in one spell at a cost of one run. His total for the series was 33 at an average of 16.42.

Against England in the Caribbean in 1993-94, Ambrose captured 4 for 58 and 4 for 37 in the second Test, and 5 for 60 and a superb 6 for 24 in the third Test. He finished with 26 wickets at an average of 19.96.

After steady performances over the next four years, against England in the Caribbean in 1997-98, Ambrose took 5 for 52 in the second innings of the second Test and 5 for 25 in the first innings of the third Test, finishing the series with 30 wickets at an average of 14.26.

On the disastrous tour of South Africa in 1998-99, Ambrose's best performance was 6 for 51 in the second innings of the second Test.

Ambrose's final series was the 2000 tour of England. He had a good series, taking 4 for 30 in the first innings of the second Test and 4 for 70 in the first innings of the third Test. In the fourth Test he took 4 for 42, including his 400th Test wicket, that of Michael Atherton, caught at slip by Brian Lara. In the fifth Test he played his last Test innings and made 28 as he bowed out of Test cricket to a standing ovation on 4 September 2000.

Ambrose also played in the English County championship for Northamptonshire, and during six seasons claimed over 300 wickets.

Ambrose retired in 2000 at the age of 37. He is attached to the Ministry of Sport in his native Antigua and Barbuda, and has been appointed roving ambassador for sport.

Curtly Elconn Lynwall Ambrose • Antigua • 1963 • Right-arm fast bowler • Left-hand batsman
Test debut: v. Pakistan at Georgetown, 1988

TESTS

Batting & Fielding	M	I	NO	Runs	HS	Ave	100	50	Ct	St
	98	145	29	1439	53	12.40	0	1	18	0

Bowling	O	M	R	W	Ave	BBI	5	10	SR	Econ
	3683.5	1001	8501	405	20.99	8-45	22	3	54.5	2.30

FIRST-CLASS (1985/86-2000)

Batting & Fielding	M	I	NO	Runs	HS	Ave	100	50	Ct	St
	239	317	70	3448	78	13.95	0	4	88	0

Bowling	O	M	R	W	Ave	BBI	5	10	SR	Econ
	8133	2262	19048	941	20.24	8-45	50	8	51.8	2.34

PETER JEFFREY LEROY DUJON

JAMAICA

The West Indies has not produced many great wicketkeepers. The best specialist 'keeper was probably the Jamaican Jackie Hendricks.
The best batsman-wicketkeeper was probably Clyde Walcott.
But the greatest West Indian wicketkeeper-batsman was Peter Jeffrey Dujon.

He was clearly the outstanding choice of his contemporaries, reflected in his being picked as wicketkeeper for the Rest of the World vs. the MCC in the latter's bicentenary match in 1987.

As a wicketkeeper Dujon was equally at ease against spinners and pace, although he was noted for his work behind the stumps against the legendary fast bowling of the Lloyd and Richards era, where his sharp reflexes and supple frame made him virtually into a slip fielder with gloves.
He was also noted for his endurance, missing only one Test in his career.

As a batsman he had a superb square drive off the front foot. Dujon usually batted down the order to consolidate his team's innings with his elegant strokeplay. He excelled against fast bowling, and his best Test innings - 139 against Australia in 1984 - was on a quick pitch at Perth.

In 81 Tests Dujon scored 3,322 runs, including five centuries, at an average of 31.94 (not bad for someone who usually batted no higher than number seven). As wicketkeeper he took 267 catches and made five stumpings. This places him third on the all-time list of dismissals behind the wicket. On three occasions he achieved 20 or moredismissals in a five-match series.

Dujon was *Wisden* Cricketer of the Year in 1989.

Dujon retired in 1991.
He was subsequently an assistant coach to the West Indies team.

CAREER HIGHLIGHTS

Dujon began his Test career on the 1981-82 tour of Australia when he played in the first two Tests as a batsman, before taking over the gloves in the third Test from David Murray at Adelaide.

His definite accession to the West Indies side took place in 1982-83 against India in the West Indies. In the fifth Test in Antigua, Dujon became the first West Indies 'keeper in over 20 years to score a century. In the first Test in Jamaica, he equalled the record for most catches in an innings (5) by a West Indies 'keeper.

On the 1983-84 tour of India, Dujon scored 367 runs at an average of 52.42 and made 16 dismissals. He sparkled with the bat on the 1983-84 tour by Australia of the Caribbean. He scored 130 in the second Test in Trinidad, averaging 40.79, and made 20 dismissals in the series.

On the West Indies tour of England in 1984, Dujon scored 101 in the fourth Test at Old Trafford, and finished up with 16 dismissals. He made 139 in the first Test at Perth against Australia in 1984-85 (19 dismissals); and 106 not out against Pakistan in 1987-88.

He had a vintage tour of England in 1988, scoring 305 runs at an average of 50.83 and accomplishing 20 dismissals. In 1988 Dujon, along with his compatriot Courtney Walsh, was awarded the Karl Nunes trophy for the outstanding West Indies cricketer during a series. In that same year he was also named Jamaica's sportsman of the year.

Against Australia in the 1990-91 series in the Caribbean, Dujon took 23 catches behind the wicket.

CAREER STATISTICS

Peter Jeffrey Leroy Dujon • Jamaica • 1956 • Wicketkeeper • Right-hand batsman
Test debut: v. Australia at Melbourne, 1981-82

TESTS

Batting & Fielding	M	I	NO	Runs	HS	Ave	100	50	Ct	St
	81	115	11	3322	139	31.94	5	16	267	5

Bowling	O	M	R	W	Ave	BBI	5	10	SR	Econ
	-	-	-	-	-	-	-	-	-	-

FIRST-CLASS (1974/75-1992/93)

Batting & Fielding	M	I	NO	Runs	HS	Ave	100	50	Ct	St
	200	298	48	9763	163*	39.05	21	50	447	22

Bowling	Balls	M	R	W	Ave	BBI	5	10	SR	Econ
	72	4	45	1	45.00	1-43	0	0	72.0	3.75

JOEL GARNER

BARBADOS

Joel 'Big Bird' Garner was one of the feared pacers who formed part of the West Indies dominance of international cricket during the Lloyd and Richards era.

While never as fast as Marshall or Holding, his height (6' 8") gave him an extraordinary bounce off the wicket, which he used to excellent advantage. Garner bowled off a short run, starting in a crouch and then rising to his full terrifying height at the moment of delivery. He bowled with immaculate control of line and length, and varied his speed and swing to good effect. He also had a notorious toe-crunching yorker.

Garner was no slouch with the bat either. A lusty hitter, his Test best was 60 against Australia (Lillee and Thompson) at Brisbane in 1979.

Garner took 259 wickets in 58 Tests at an average of 20.97, with a strike rate of 50.80 that places him among the top Test bowlers of all time. He took more than 25 wickets in a series on five occasions.

Garner's One-Day International career was equally striking. Often required to bowl 'at the death' (the critical last couple of overs), he was rarely expensive, and often miserly. 146 wickets, at an economy rate of 3.09 and an average of 18.84 with a best of 5-31 against Australia in 1984, show just how effective he was.

Garner was *Wisden* Cricketer of the Year in 1980. He was awarded the MBE in 1985 for his services to cricket.

After retirement, he has remained involved in cricket as a selector for the West Indies Cricket Board and a manager of the West Indies 'A' team. He has served on the board of the Barbados Cricket Association, and as a technical officer with the Barbados Sports Council.

CAREER HIGHLIGHTS

Joel Garner made his debut in 1977 in the first Test against Pakistan at Bridgetown, after Michael Holding and Wayne Daniel were injured. He took 4 for 130 in the first innings. He finished the series with 25 wickets at an average of 27.52, including 4 for 48 and 4 for 100 in the third Test in Guyana.

In 1978, when Australia toured the Caribbean, Garner took four wickets in each innings of the second Test in Barbados. Garner then joined most of the West Indies team to play in Kerry Packer's World Series Cricket in Australia where he was a star performer.

It took Garner a while to earn the new ball. He was at first used as second change in a pace attack that included Roberts, Holding, Croft and later Marshall. In the 1979 World Cup, Garner, a great one for the big occasion, played a key role in the victory over England in the final, taking 5 for 38, including 4 wickets for 4 runs in 11 balls.

After 1979 Garner became a permanent fixture in the West Indies team. He was instrumental in the West Indies winning their first Test series in Australia in 1979-80, leading the bowling averages. Garner had a great series against England in 1980, taking 26 wickets at an average of 14.26, with two 4-wicket hauls in the first and second Tests.

This was followed by commendable performances against Pakistan, England, Australia and India. Due to a shoulder injury in 1983, Garner took a rest from cricket, but came back the following year for the World Series One-Day tournament in Australia. Though experiencing problems with his knees, he appeared in the three final matches and took 10 for 89 in 29 overs.

During the Australian tour of the Caribbean in 1983-84, a fully fit Garner, opening the bowling in the absence of Holding and Marshall, took 31 wickets at an average of 16.87, with performances of 6 for 75 in the first Test in Guyana, 6 for 60 in the second Test in Trinidad, and 5 for 63 in the fourth Test in Antigua. He was Man-of-the-Series and the main reason why West Indies won that rubber 3-0.

In the West Indies 5-0 'blackwash' series against England in 1984, Garner headed the wickets taken with 29 at 18.62 apiece, as he wreaked havoc with his awkward bounce. In the first Test he took 4 for 53 and 5 for 55.

He followed up with a strong tour of Australia in 1984-85 and against England in the Caribbean in 1985-86. On that occasion he captured 27 wickets (16.14).

At the end of the New Zealand tour in 1987, in which he topped the bowling averages, Garner retired from Test cricket at the age of 35. He played in the English County championship for Somerset, starting in 1977. He also played for Western Australia in 1982-83.

CAREER STATISTICS

Joel Garner • Barbados • 1952 • Right-arm fast bowler • Right-hand batsman
Test debut: v. Pakistan at Bridgetown, 1977

TESTS

Batting & Fielding	M	I	NO	Runs	HS	Ave	100	50	Ct	St
	58	68	14	672	60	12.44	0	1	42	0

Bowling	O	M	R	W	Ave	BBI	5	10	SR	Econ
	2195.5	576	5433	259	20.97	6-56	7	0	50.8	2.47

FIRST-CLASS (1971-1993)

Batting & Fielding	M	I	NO	Runs	HS	Ave	100	50	Ct	St
	214	231	54	2964	104	16.74	1	8	129	0

Bowling	Balls	M	R	W	Ave	BBI	5	10	SR	Econ
	39829	1794	16333	881	18.53	8-31	48	7	45.2	2.46

CUTHBERT GORDON GREENIDGE

BARBADOS

Gordon Greenidge and Desmond Haynes were arguably the best pair of opening batsmen in post-war cricket, if not ever. They are certain to be ranked in the company of Hobbs and Sutcliffe, Hutton and Washbrook, Simpson and Lawry. Certainly they were the longest and most successful opening partnership in the history of West Indies cricket.

The statistics show that in 89 Tests together and 148 partnerships (11 unbroken) they amassed a total of 6,483 runs. Of those 89 Tests the West Indies won 48, lost 8 and drew 33. They exceeded a century on 16 occasions, and fifty a further 26 times. Their average opening partnership was 47.32, the best being 298 against England in Antigua in 1990.

A brilliant, aggressive batsman, Greenidge was a powerful striker of the ball on both sides of the wicket. He had a magnificent hook and savage square cut, two invaluable weapons in the armoury of an opening bat. He also had a liking for hitting sixes. He twice hit 13 sixes in an innings in his first-class career. At the same time he had a sound defensive technique. He was undoubtedly the greatest opening batsman the West Indies ever had.

In 108 Tests, Greenidge amassed 7,558 runs at an average of 44.72. He scored 19 Test centuries (four of them doubles).

Greenidge was also an excellent slip fielder. He held 96 catches. He was *Wisden* Cricketer of the Year in 1977.

After he retired, Greenidge remained involved in cricket. He has been a member of the West Indies Panel of Selectors. He was national coach of the Bangladesh team for a while.

Greenidge and Haynes have given their name to a stand at Kensington Oval.

CAREER HIGHLIGHTS

Although born and raised in Barbados, Greenidge emigrated to England when he was ten, and spent his formative cricket years in England where he was selected for the South of England's schoolboys cricket team.

In 1970 Greenidge began opening the batting for Hampshire with the great South African batsman, Barry Richards. It was while playing for Hampshire that Greenidge's prolific scoring caught the eye of the Barbados selectors who invited him back home to play in the regional competition.

Greenidge started his Test career in 1974 at the age of 23 with a bang, against India at Bangalore. He made 93 and 107 in the two innings and became the eighth West Indian to score a century in his debut Test.

Two years later, in 1976, Greenidge enjoyed a great tour of England. He scored 84 in the second Test at Lord's, and two centuries on a difficult pitch in the third Test at Old Trafford. In the fourth Test at Headingley he also scored a century and had 85 not out in the final Test at The Oval. He ended the tour with 592 Test runs at an average of 65.77.

Against Pakistan in the Caribbean in 1977, Greenidge scored 70 in the second Test in Trinidad, 91 and 96 in the third match in Guyana, and a century in the fifth Test in Jamaica, amassing 536 runs at an average of 53.60.

After a lean patch, Greenidge returned to form against India in the Caribbean in 1982-83, scoring his first Test century in six years, with 154 retired not out in the fifth Test in Antigua. In the first Test against Australia in the Caribbean in 1983-84, he made 120 not out and in the fifth Test 127.

Greenidge then followed this up with a magnificent tour of England in 1984. One of his finest innings under pressure was in the second Test at Lord's with the West Indies needing 342 to win on the final day. Greenidge scored an unbeaten double century in an unbroken stand of 287 with Larry Gomes. The 214 came off 242 balls with two sixes and 29 fours. In the fourth Test at Old Trafford Greenidge scored 223, including 30 fours. This performance helped to rescue the West Indies from defeat. He ended the tour with 572 runs at an average of 81.71.

In 1987 he enjoyed a good tour of New Zealand, hitting 213 in the second Test at Auckland and topping the batting averages for the tour.

In the 1990 series against England in the Caribbean, Greenidge scored 149 in a superb partnership with Haynes of 298 (their best) in Antigua.

After a good series against Australia in 1991, during which he made his highest Test score of 226 (including 32 fours) in the fourth Test in Barbados, Greenidge retired at the age of forty.

Cuthbert Gordon Greenidge • Barbados • 1951 • Right-hand opening batsman • Occasional right-arm slow medium bowler
Test debut: v. India at Bangalore, 1974/75

TESTS

Batting & Fielding	M	I	NO	Runs	HS	Ave	100	50	Ct	St
	108	185	16	7558	226	44.72	19	34	96	0

Bowling	Balls	M	R	W	Ave	BBI	5	10	SR	Econ
	26	3	4	0	-	-	0	0	-	0.92

FIRST-CLASS (1970-1992)

Batting & Fielding	M	I	NO	Runs	HS	Ave	100	50	Ct	St
	523	889	75	37354	273*	45.88	92	183	516	0

Bowling	Balls	M	R	W	Ave	BBI	5	10	SR	Econ
	955	41	479	18	26.49	5-49	1	0	53.0	3.00

DESMOND LEO HAYNES

BARBADOS

Desmond Haynes was the other half of the most successful West Indian batting partnership ever. He and Gordon Greenidge were the bane of bowlers the world over for almost thirteen years.

One can get into serious arguments about whether they were the best opening pair ever; but the statistics show that in 89 Tests together, 148 partnerships - 11 unbroken - they amassed a total of 6,483 runs, nearly 3,000 more than the next opening pair on the ladder, Lawry and Simpson of Australia. Of those 89 Tests the West Indies won 48, lost 8 and drew 33. They exceeded a century on 16 occasions, and fifty a further 26 times. Their average opening partnership was 47.32, the best being 298 against England in Antigua in 1990.

While Greenidge was the more aggressive of the two, Haynes could set about the bowling when he was ready with a flourish which made Greenidge look like a tortoise. He was strong on the leg side, but developed a beautiful cover drive and became a master of the late cut.

Haynes' usual role was that of sheet anchor in a team of aggressive batsmen that included Greenidge, Richards and Lloyd.

Haynes played in 116 Tests, scoring 7,487 runs, including 18 centuries at an average of 42.29. He was *Wisden* Cricketer of the Year in 1991.

Haynes had what many consider to be a raw deal towards the end of his career. Although he served as vice-captain under Richards, he was overlooked and Richardson was appointed captain after Richards retired.

Later he had a major disagreement with the West Indies Cricket Board in 1995 when they ruled that he was ineligible to play in the home series against Australia because he had missed one match in the regional competition due to a contract he had with Western Province in South Africa. This was one of those errors of judgment that hastened the decline of the West Indies' cricketing fortunes.

Haynes finished his first-class career in 1997, playing for Western Province in South Africa. He was appointed a senator in the Barbados Parliament in 2001.

CAREER HIGHLIGHTS

Desmond Haynes came into the West Indies team after Fredericks retired in 1977, in the home series against Australia in 1977-78. In the first Test in Trinidad he hit 61 and top scored with 66 in the first innings of the second Test in Barbados. He and Greenidge added 131 in the second innings to lead the West Indies to victory.

Like many other West Indies cricketers, Haynes went off to Australia in 1978, midway through the series against Australia, to join the Packer World Series. In his first One-Day International against Australia in the Caribbean in 1978, Haynes hit a masterful 148 off 136 balls.

After the World Series hiatus, Haynes and Greenidge formed their enduring partnership. On the tour of New Zealand in 1979-80, Haynes scored 55 and 105 in the first Test, and 122 in the second Test. On the 1980 tour of England he hit 184 in the second Test at Lord's, occupying the crease for 490 minutes, proving he had the necessary powers of concentration. This was one of his finest innings.

On the England tour of the Caribbean in 1980-81 he scored 96 in the first Test in Trinidad, and 84 in the fifth Test in Jamaica. Haynes' next great innings were against India in the Caribbean in 1982-83. He made 92 in the fourth Test in Barbados and 136 in the final Test in Antigua in a magnificent partnership of 298 with Greenidge.

Haynes had a superb series against Australia in the Caribbean in 1983-84. He scored 486 runs (average 93.66), including 60 and an unbeaten 103 in the first Test in Guyana; 53 in the second Test in Trinidad; 145 in the third Test in Barbados; and 60 and 15 not out in the final Test in Jamaica.

Haynes' next good series was against New Zealand in 1984-85 when he scored 78, 90, 62 and 76 in the four Tests. He then had a fantastic series against England in the Caribbean in 1985-86, when he averaged 78.16 with a century in the fifth Test in Antigua. He had a great tour of Australia in 1988-89, scoring 537 runs at an average of 59.66 and making two centuries. He hit two more centuries against England in the Caribbean in 1990.

Against Pakistan in the Caribbean in 1993, Haynes scored the last two centuries in his Test career. His last Test for the West Indies was the fourth match against England in Barbados in the 1993-94 series.

Desmond Leo Haynes • Barbados • 1956 • Right-hand opening batsman • Right-arm leg break, medium bowler
Test debut: v. Australia at Port-of-Spain, 1977-78

TESTS

Batting & Fielding	M	I	NO	Runs	HS	Ave	100	50	Ct	St
	116	202	25	7487	184	42.29	18	39	65	0

Bowling	O	M	R	W	Ave	BBI	5	10	SR	Econ
	3	0	8	1	8.00	1-2	0	0	18.0	2.66

FIRST-CLASS (1976/77-1996/97)

Batting & Fielding	M	I	NO	Runs	HS	Ave	100	50	Ct	St
	376	639	72	26030	255*	45.90	61	138	202	1

Bowling	Balls	M	R	W	Ave	BBI	5	10	SR	Econ
	536	24	279	8	34.87	1-2	0	0	67.0	3.12

MICHAEL HOLDING

JAMAICA

Holding had one of the smoothest and most beautiful actions of all fast bowlers. He had balance, rhythm and a long, flowing, quiet run up, which, coupled with the terrifying speed of his deliveries, earned him the nicknames 'Whispering Death' and the 'Rolls Royce of Fast Bowlers'. He was a joy to watch and a terror to face.

He was undoubtedly one of the best and fastest pace bowlers the West Indies ever produced, and one of the most outstanding in the world. By now, the over he bowled to England's opener, Geoff Boycott, in the third Test of the 1980-81 series at Kensington Oval is the stuff of legend. Operating from the northern end he demoralised Boycott with the first five deliveries of torrid pace and control and then bowled him, backing away, for a duck.

Holding's 8 for 92 and a match haul of 14 for 149 against England on a lifeless pitch at The Oval in London in 1976 was one of the all-time great bowling performances.

Holding took 249 wickets in 60 Tests at an average of 23.68. He was *Wisden* Cricketer of the Year in 1977.

Since retiring Holding has been a regular cricket commentator and writer. In 2003 he was appointed ambassador-at-large by the government of Jamaica.

CAREER HIGHLIGHTS

Holding began his Test career on the West Indies tour of Australia in 1975-76, as a partner to Andy Roberts. In the second Test at Perth he took 4 for 88 including three wickets in the second over on the second day, but injury plagued him for the rest of the tour. It was during that tour that Roberts and Holding became the foundation of the West Indies famous four-pronged pace attack.

Against India in the West Indies in 1976 Holding headed the bowling averages with 19 wickets at an average of 19.89, including 6 for 65 in the third Test in Trinidad. In the fourth Test in Jamaica he took 4 for 82. The Indians complained of intimidatory bowling, with five of their batsmen 'absent hurt', which enhanced Holding's reputation. As Holding explained in *The Cricketer* in 1985: 'I want him [the batsman] to be aware that if he gets onto the front foot against me he might find himself in trouble - in other words he might get hurt.'

On the West Indies tour of England in 1976 Holding and Roberts devastated the English batting with 28 wickets apiece for the series (Holding with a miserly average of 12.71). In the third Test at Old Trafford, Holding took 5 for 9 in 7.5 overs in England's second innings to lead the West Indies to victory. In the fifth Test at The Oval he took 14 match wickets with 8 for 92 in the second innings.

After this great summer in England, Holding suffered from injuries and then went off to the Packer World Series Cricket. On his return in 1980, he took 6 for 67 in the second Test at Lord's. Playing in the three-Test series against Australia in the Caribbean in 1981-82, Holding took 24 wickets at 14.33 each. On the 1983-84 tour of India, Holding, bowling in tandem with Marshall, took 30 wickets at an average of 22.10.

In the 1984-85 series against Australia, Holding produced a superb spell of bowling in the first Test at Perth to take 6 for 21 in 35 balls, dismissing the Aussies for their lowest total against the West Indies: 76.

In the 1986 series against England in the Caribbean, the injury-hampered veteran got 16 at an average of 16.04. His last tour was to New Zealand in 1987.

Michael Holding • Jamaica • 1954 • Right-arm fast bowler • Right-hand batsman
Test debut: v. Australia at Brisbane, 1975-76

TESTS

Batting & Fielding	M	I	NO	Runs	HS	Ave	100	50	Ct	St
	60	76	10	910	73	13.78	0	6	22	0

Bowling	Balls	M	R	W	Ave	BBI	5	10	SR	Econ
	12680	459	5898	249	23.68	8-92	13	2	50.9	2.79

FIRST-CLASS (1972/73-1989)

Batting & Fielding	M	I	NO	Runs	HS	Ave	100	50	Ct	St
	222	283	43	3600	80	15.00	0	14	125	0

Bowling	Balls	M	R	W	Ave	BBI	5	10	SR	Econ
	38877	1452	18233	778	23.43	8-92	39	5	49.9	2.81

ALVIN ISAAC KALLICHARRAN

GUYANA

Alvin Kallicharran is probably one of the more underrated West Indian batsmen. He was often compared and contrasted with the elegant Jamaican batsman, Lawrence Rowe. Unlike Rowe, Kallicharran was a left-hander, but equally stylish.

He was a touch player with near perfect timing, and a wide selection of shots. His footwork was nimble and he was a master cutter and puller of the ball. He was a superb player of spin. Like Rowe he scored a century on his Test debut. He was also a great slip fielder, taking 51 catches in Tests.

Kallicharran scored an aggregate of 4,399 runs, including 12 centuries and 21 half centuries, at an average of 44.43 in 66 Tests.

Kallicharran was *Wisden* Cricketer of the Year in 1983.

After the 1980-81 tour of Pakistan, Kallicharran provoked an uproar with his decision to be the first West Indies cricketer to play in South Africa, when he joined Transvaal in 1981-82. Banned from the West Indies team, he played County cricket in England with success, scoring over 2,000 runs in 1982, including three double and five single centuries. He also played in Australia.

After retiring, Kallicharran remained involved in cricket, including coaching the Kenyan national cricket team.

CAREER HIGHLIGHTS

Kallicharran began his Test career in style, scoring 100 not out against New Zealand in the fourth Test in Guyana in 1972. In the fifth Test in Trinidad, just to show it was no fluke, he scored 101.

He followed this with a solid 1972-73 series against Australia in the Caribbean, and on the tour to England in 1973 he finished with an average of 64.78.

He had a great series against England in the Caribbean in 1974, scoring 158 in the first Test in Trinidad, 93 in the second Test in Jamaica, and 119 in the third Test in Barbados, sharing a record second-wicket partnership of 249 with Lawrence Rowe who scored a magnificent 302.

He performed brilliantly on the West Indies tour of India and Pakistan in 1974-75. In the first Test in Bangalore he scored a century, and in the deciding game at Bombay he made 98 to help clinch the series for the West Indies. In the first Test at Lahore against Pakistan Kallicharran scored 92 not out, and in the final Test at Karachi he scored 115.

On the disastrous 1975 West Indies tour of Australia (1-5), Kallicharran stood up to the blistering pace of Lillee and Thompson, scoring a century in the first Test at Brisbane, and 57 in the second Test at Perth despite having his nose broken by a ball in the match. He got another two fifties in the final Test at Adelaide.

Kallicharran was one of the first to sign up for the Kerry Packer World Series in 1977. But he subsequently withdrew and captained the depleted official West Indies side for the remainder of the Test series against the Australians in the Caribbean in 1977-78 after the West Indians contracted to Packer withdrew on the eve of the third Test. He performed well, scoring 92 and 69 in the fourth Test in Trinidad and a century in the final game in Jamaica.

Kallicharran continued to captain the West Indies on the subsequent tour of India, in 1978-79, scoring 538 runs at an average of 59.77, but was dropped as captain when the Packer players returned for the tours to Australia and New Zealand in 1979-80. He made a century against Australia in the third Test at Adelaide; and 75 and 46 in the second and third Tests in New Zealand.

The 1980-81 tour of Pakistan was his last series for the West Indies.

Alvin Isaac Kallicharran • Guyana • 1949 • Left-hand batsman • Right-arm off-break bowler
Test debut: v. New Zealand at Georgetown, 1972

TESTS

Batting & Fielding	M	I	NO	Runs	HS	Ave	100	50	Ct	St
	66	109	10	4399	187	44.43	12	21	51	0

Bowling	Balls	M	R	W	Ave	BBI	5	10	SR	Econ
	406	14	158	4	39.50	2-16	0	0	101.5	2.33

FIRST-CLASS (1966/67-1990)

Batting & Fielding	M	I	NO	Runs	HS	Ave	100	50	Ct	St
	505	834	86	32650	243*	43.64	87	160	323	0

Bowling	Balls	M	R	W	Ave	BBI	5	10	SR	Econ
	-	-	4030	84	47.97	5-45	1	0	-	-

CLIVE HUBERT LLOYD

GUYANA

Clive Lloyd was a vicious striker of the ball. His heavy bat, powerful shoulders and full swing of the arms could destroy the opponents' bowling in a flash. He could cut, hook and drive with unrelenting ferocity.

His height (6' 5") gave him tremendous reach, which he used to advantage in smothering awkward balls when playing spin. At the same time he did not hesitate to step down the pitch and loft spinners into the deep.

He was a useful medium pace bowler, taking 114 first-class and 10 Test wickets, and one of the best cover fielders in the game, until injury forced him to move to the slips where he took many of his 90 Test catches.

Clive Lloyd will, however, go down in history as the man who, more than anyone else, contributed to the rise of West Indian cricket to world supremacy for almost two decades. He was the longest-serving and most successful Test captain of all time. He led the West Indies in a record 74 Tests from 1975 to 1985, establishing the team as the powerhouse of international cricket. This included 26 consecutive Tests without a defeat and 11 successive victories. He had a record 36 victories.

Many players have found the captaincy a burden that inhibits their own game. Not Lloyd. He had a higher batting average for the period when he was captain. He made 14 of his 19 centuries while leading the West Indies.

Lloyd made the following comment on his captaincy: 'It was the professionalism and togetherness, players realising the importance of what they had to do and their commitment. These guys were totally West Indian in everything they did.'

Lloyd accumulated 7,515 runs, including 19 centuries and 39 fifties, in 110 Tests at an average of 46.67. He was *Wisden* Cricketer of the Year in 1971.

After retiring Lloyd remained involved with cricket, both in Guyana and internationally. He managed the West Indies team after their disappointing showing in the 1996 World Cup until 1999.

Lloyd has also served as an ICC match referee. He now lives in England.

CAREER HIGHLIGHTS

Lloyd began his Test career in 1966 against India in the first Test at Bombay. He scored 82 in the first innings and 78 not out in the second, helping his team to victory.

On the 1967-68 tour by England of the Caribbean Lloyd scored his first Test century - a thrilling 118 - in the first Test in Trinidad, and a commanding 113 not out in the third Test in Barbados.

One of Lloyd's great innings was against the touring Australians in 1973, when he struck a brilliant 178, including one six and 24 fours, in the fourth Test in Guyana. On the short tour of England in 1973, he scored a dashing 132 in the first Test at The Oval, followed up with 94 in the second Test at Edgbaston, ending the series with an average of 63.60.

Lloyd was appointed captain for the tour to India and Pakistan in 1974-75. He had a magnificent series. In the first Test at Bangalore he scored a lightning 163 (reaching his 100 off 85 balls), followed by 71 in the second Test at Delhi, and in the last game at Bombay he scored a career best of 242 not out. His aggregate for the tour, 636, at an average of 79.20, was his highest in any series, and was instrumental in the West Indies winning the series 3-2.

In the 1975 World Cup he hit a match-winning century in the final.

One of the turning points in Lloyd's career and the West Indies' fortunes was the disastrous 1975-76 tour of Australia. The West Indies were simply overwhelmed by the pace of Lillee and Thompson, and although Lloyd excelled with the bat, scoring 1 49 in the second Test at Perth and 102 and 91 not out in the two Tests at Melbourne, the West Indies lost the series 5-1.

It was at this point that Lloyd decided that the key to the West Indies winning was to have a quality four-pronged pace attack. This in fact, along with superb batting and the professionalism and determination that Lloyd instilled in the team, became the basis of West Indies dominance of the game for almost two decades. It changed the way cricket was played.

Midway through the 1977-78 series against Australia in the Caribbean, Lloyd and most of the West Indies players left to play in the Packer World Series. This was also a formative experience for the future West Indies team. Lloyd returned in 1979 to lead the West Indies to victory in the World Cup.

On the short tour of Australia in 1979-80, Lloyd hit a brilliant 121 in the final Test at Adelaide, to achieve the West Indies' first ever series win in Australia, 2-0.

Lloyd had a great series with the bat against India in the Caribbean in 1983. He scored a thrilling 143 in the second Test in Trinidad, and a century in the final Test in Antigua, leading the West Indies to a 2-0 victory.

After the shock of losing the 1983 World Cup to India - which Lloyd considered his greatest disappointment - he got his revenge by defeating India in the One-Day series 5-0 and the Test series 3-0. Lloyd topped the Test averages with 82.66, including two centuries.

On the Australian tour of the Caribbean in 1984 the Australians failed to win a single game. In the summer of the same year the West Indies trounced England at home 5-0, achieving eleven consecutive victories.

On the 1984-85 tour of Australia, Lloyd also led the West Indies to victory, contributing 114 in the second Test at Brisbane, 78 in the third Test at Adelaide, and 72 on a difficult pitch at Sydney. After that series Lloyd retired.

Lloyd had a distinguished career playing in the Lancashire League and later - in 1969 - for the County side. He helped Lancashire win the Gillette Cup four times between 1970 and 1975. He was appointed captain of Lancashire in 1981.

Clive Hubert Lloyd • Guyana • 1944 • Left-hand batsman • Right-arm medium pace bowler
Test debut: v. India at Bombay, 1966

TESTS

Batting & Fielding	M	I	NO	Runs	HS	Ave	100	50	Ct	St
	110	175	14	7515	242*	46.67	19	39	90	0

Bowling	Balls	M	R	W	Ave	BBI	5	10	SR	Econ
	1716	75	622	10	62.20	2-13	0	0	171.6	2.17

FIRST-CLASS (1963/64-1986)

Batting & Fielding	M	I	NO	Runs	HS	Ave	100	50	Ct	St
	490	730	96	31232	242	49.26	79	172	377	0

Bowling	Balls	M	R	W	Ave	BBI	5	10	SR	Econ
	9551	379	4104	114	36.00	4-88	0	0	83.7	2.57

MALCOLM DENZIL MARSHALL

BARBADOS

Malcolm 'Maco' Marshall was arguably the best of the great West Indies fast bowlers of the 70s and 80s during the period of West Indies domination of the cricketing world. He was certainly the most successful.

Some even rank him as the finest ever West Indies fast bowler and one of the six greatest fast bowlers of all time. His 376 Test wickets at an average of 20.94 in 81 Tests testify to his greatness. He took more than 25 wickets in a series on five occasions. On four occasions he took 10 or more wickets in a Test, and he took a wicket every 46.77 balls.

Although relatively short (5' 10") for a fast bowler, Marshall had the ability to generate lethal pace because of his quick run up and whippy arm action. He was genuinely fast, and his deadly accurate bouncers were feared by batsmen the world over.

Marshall bowled a consistently good line and length and was able to swing the ball prodigiously, and late, and cut it with great subtlety, because of his grip and unusual action. At times he was virtually unplayable. He also had great stamina for a strike bowler.

Marshall was a good batsman, and in a team less blessed with fine batsman he might have developed into an all-rounder of class, but he invariably came too low down the order. He made 10 Test fifties and his highest score was 92, against India at Kanpur in 1983.

Marshall was *Wisden* Cricketer of the Year in 1983.
After he retired, Marshall was the coach of the West Indies team until his death from cancer in 1999.

Marshall made his Test debut on the West Indies 1978-79 tour of India, in the second Test at Bangalore. But a nagging back injury delayed the full impact of this devastating bowler until 1983, when in the series against India in the Caribbean, Marshall took 21 wickets at an average of 23.57, including 5 for 37 in the second Test in Trinidad.

He thereafter became a permanent member of the feared four-pronged West Indies pace attack, and was recognised as the fastest bowler in the world at the time. He enjoyed a hugely successful series on the West Indies tour of India in 1983-84, taking 33 wickets at a cost of 18.81 each. He took four wickets in both innings of the Test at Kanpur and also slammed 92 runs. In the fifth Test at Calcutta he sliced through the Indian side, taking 6 for 37. In the sixth Test at Madras he took 5 for 72.

After a good series at home against Australia in 1983-84 and against England in England in 1984, Marshall continued his lethal performance in the 1984-85 series against Australia. He took 5 wickets in an innings on four successive occasions, and dismissed ten batsmen in the third Test at Adelaide. He finished the series with 28 wickets at an average of 19.78, winning the Man-of-the-Series award, which he also won in his next two series.

On England's tour of the Caribbean in 1986 he broke Gatting's nose in the first One-Day match, and in the Test series he took 27 wickets at an average of 17.85. He also performed well with the bat. In the second Test in Trinidad he took his 200th wicket.

Marshall did not let up in the following series against Pakistan and New Zealand, and had a fantastic series in 1988 against England, taking 6 for 69 in the first Test; 6 for 32 and 4 for 60 in the second Test; and 2 for 19 and 7 for 22 in the third Test, ending the series with 35 wickets at an average of 12.65!

In the third Test against Australia in 1988-89, Marshall took his 300th Test wicket. In early 1989 he took 5 for 60 in the second Test against India, and 5 for 34 and 6 for 55 in the third Test.

After the 1991 series against England, Marshall retired in 1992. Marshall also played and coached fourteen seasons for Hampshire and for Natal province in South Africa.

Malcolm Denzil Marshall • Barbados • 1958-1999 • Right-arm fast bowler • Right-hand batsman
Test debut: v. India at Bangalore, 1978

TESTS

Batting & Fielding	M	I	NO	Runs	HS	Ave	100	50	Ct	St
	81	107	11	1810	92	18.85	0	10	25	0

Bowling	O	M	R	W	Ave	BBI	5	10	SR	Econ
	2930.4	613	7876	376	20.94	7-22	22	4	46.7	2.68

FIRST-CLASS (1977/78-1995/96)

Batting & Fielding	M	I	NO	Runs	HS	Ave	100	50	Ct	St
	408	516	73	11004	120*	24.83	7	54	145	0

Bowling	Balls	M	R	W	Ave	BBI	5	10	SR	Econ
	74645	3180	31548	1651	19.10	8-71	85	13	45.2	2.53

SIR
VIVIAN RICHARDS

ANTIGUA

Isaac Vivian Alexander Richards, better known as the 'Master Blaster', is regarded as the finest batsman of his generation, one of the greatest West Indies batsmen, and in the top six of the greatest batsmen of all time. He was named in *Wisden 2000*, along with Don Bradman, Jack Hobbs, Garfield Sobers and Shane Warne, as one of the five cricketers of the century.

Moreover, Richards had something that seems sadly lacking in West Indies cricket today: a fierce pride in the West Indian 'nation' and an understanding of what cricket means to the West Indian people. This gave him a strong and ruthless desire to win which rubbed off on his team mates.

At 5' 11" Richards was strong, supremely confident and an aggressive hitter of the ball on either side of the wicket. He had every orthodox stroke at his command and his timing and footwork were magical. But it was his unorthodox shots which made most bowlers despair. His ability to plant his left foot outside off stump and drive a ball pitched on the off side through mid-on was astonishing. His lightning-fast reflexes and strength made up for his unconventional technique. He could flick a four or a six to midwicket with effortless ease.

He had punishing power and always tried to dominate the bowling in an arrogantly dismissive manner.

He refused to wear a helmet and particularly loved destroying fast bowling. It was said that even great opposition bowlers squirmed when he swaggered to the crease.

On one occasion when Richards was representing Somerset, Glamorgan's Greg Thomas once made Richards play and miss three times. The bowler turned to Richards and said: 'It's red, it's round and you're supposed to hit it.' Richards clubbed the next ball out of the ground for six and said: 'You know what it looks like. Now go and find it.'

Richards was also a competent off-spinner and a brilliant cover point and slip fielder. He took 122 Test catches.

Richards took over the captaincy of the West Indies team from Clive Lloyd in the mid-1980s and is the only West Indies captain never to have lost a series. Under his captaincy, the West Indies won 27, drew 15 and lost only 8 out of 50 Tests.

Richards amassed 8,540 runs, including 24 centuries and 45 half centuries, in 121 Tests at an impressive average of 50.23 and became the first West Indian cricketer to score one hundred first-class 100s. He holds the record for the most Test sixes (84). He was *Wisden* Cricketer of the Year in 1977.

After his retirement, Richards remained actively involved in West Indies cricket. He was appointed coach of the West Indies team for the 1999-2000 tour of New Zealand, and is presently Chairman of Selectors of the West Indies Cricket Board. Richards was knighted in 1999 for his services to cricket, and is an ambassador-at-large for Antigua and Barbuda. He was conferred with an honorary degree of Doctor of Laws by the University of the West Indies in 2000.

CAREER HIGHLIGHTS

Viv Richards began his Test career on the 1973-74 tour of India and Pakistan. He immediately showed his prowess by hitting 192 not out in the second Test at Delhi. He had a great series against India in the Caribbean in 1975-76. He scored 142 in the first Test in Barbados, 130 in the second Test in Trinidad and 177 in the fourth match in Jamaica, amassing 556 runs at an average of 92.66.

It was on the following tour of England in 1976 that Richards came of age as the dominant force in batting in the world. He was at his vicious best, following an unfortunate comment by the South African-born captain of the England team, Tony Greig, that he would make the West Indies grovel. Richards ransacked the English bowling. In the first Test at Trent Bridge he scored 232, an innings described by one commentator as 'cultured violence'.

Richards followed this up with a brilliant 291 in the fifth Test at The Oval. This innings has been compared with Headley's 270 not out in Jamaica against England in 1935, Worrell's 261 against England in 1950, and Sobers' 254 for the Rest of the World at Melbourne against Australia in 1972 as one of the greatest innings ever played by a West Indian. Richards amassed from four Tests 829 runs at an average of 118.42! Alec Bedser wrote that there was a question of whether he was 'a bludgeoning murderer or a clinical assassin'.

After the Packer World Series, Richards had a solid tour of Australia and New Zealand in 1979-80, followed by the 1980 tour of England. He scored a dazzling 145 in the second Test at Lord's including a six and 25 fours. He finished the series as leading West Indies batsman in both Test and first-class matches.

Against England in the Caribbean in 1980-81, Richards hit a brilliant 182 not out in the second innings of the third Test in Barbados, and 114 in the fourth Test in Antigua, the first ever held there.

After good series against India and Australia, Richards returned to the scene of his earlier triumphs in England in 1984. He scored 117 in the first Test at Edgbaston, and 189 off 170 balls in the first One-Day International at Old Trafford. It was then the highest innings in One-Day cricket and included 5 sixes and 21 fours. He made the runs out of a total of 272 after the West Indies' ninth wicket had fallen at 161. Many still consider it the finest One-Day innings ever.

On the tour of Australia in 1984-85, Richards scored a superb 208 with three sixes and 22 fours in the fourth Test at Melbourne. He also scored 58 on a difficult wicket in the last Test at Sydney.

After Lloyd's retirement Richards was appointed captain for the series against New Zealand in the Caribbean in 1985. He scored two fifties in the first Test in Trinidad, and a century in the third and final Test in Barbados to clinch the series for the West Indies.

He also led the West Indies to a 5-0 drubbing of England in the Caribbean in 1987. He finished the series with an average of 66.20 and had a brilliant century in the fifth Test in Antigua. It was the fastest in the history of Test cricket, coming off 56 deliveries in 81 minutes.

After 1988, Richards' mercurially brilliant batting fell off, with only the occasional century coming from his bat. Yet he played vital innings and led his team with great success, including a 4-0 rout of England in 1988. Richards retired after the 1991 tour to England.

Richards also played for Somerset in the English County championship between 1974 and 1986, helping them to win the Gillette Cup and the John Player Sunday League title in 1979. He ended his County career playing for Glamorgan between 1990 and 1993.

Sir Vivian Richards • Antigua • 1952 • Right-hand batsman • Right-arm off-spinner and medium pace bowler
Test debut: v. India at Bangalore, 1974-75

TESTS

Batting & Fielding	M	I	NO	Runs	HS	Ave	100	50	Ct	St
	121	182	12	8540	291	50.23	24	45	122	0

Bowling	Balls	M	R	W	Ave	BBI	5	10	SR	Econ
	5170	203	1964	32	61.37	2-17	0	0	161.5	2.27

FIRST-CLASS (1971-1993)

Batting & Fielding	M	I	NO	Runs	HS	Ave	100	50	Ct	St
	507	796	63	36212	322	49.40	114	162	464	1

Bowling	Balls	M	R	W	Ave	BBI	5	10	SR	Econ
	23220	942	10070	223	45.15	5-88	1	0	104.1	2.60

ANDERSON MONTGOMERY EVERTON ROBERTS

ANTIGUA

Andy Roberts, 6' 2", was the first of the feared quartet of fast bowlers to catapult the West Indies to the top of international cricket in the 1970s. Roberts and Holding used to bowl in tandem, and rank with the most dreaded pair of pace bowlers in the world. And when you realise that following them were Marshall and Garner, it was enough to give any opposing batsman the shakes.

Roberts had blistering pace, with an explosive and well-concealed bouncer. He was also deadly accurate, often seaming the ball into the batsman. He had a straight, easy run up before he exploded into action and released the ball fast and straight.

Roberts took 5 wickets in an innings eleven times and twice had 10 or more wickets in a match. He took 100 Test wickets in a record time of 2 years and 142 days. Overall, he took 202 Test wickets at an average of 25.61 in 47 Tests.

Roberts was *Wisden* Cricketer of the Year in 1975. After he retired, he served as a coach to the West Indies team and a sports officer for the government of Antigua and Barbuda.

CAREER HIGHLIGHTS

Roberts became the first Antiguan to play for the West Indies when he made his Test debut in 1974 against England in the third Test in Barbados. But he failed to maintain his place after struggling on a docile wicket.

Following his Test debut, he had a season of County cricket in England where he honed his skills, collecting 119 wickets at an average of 13.62 from 21 games. Roberts blossomed on the West Indies tour of India in 1974-75. He ended up with 32 wickets at an average of 18.28, including 5 for 50 in the third Test at Calcutta and match figures of 12 for 121 in the fourth Test at Madras.

On the disastrous West Indies 1975-76 tour of Australia, Roberts finished as the leading wicket-taker with 22 at an average of 26.32. In the second Test at Perth - the only one won by the West Indies - he took the first seven wickets in the second innings for 54 runs.

Roberts had a superb tour of England in 1976. In the second Test he became the first West Indian to take ten wickets in a Test at Lord's. In the third Test at Old Trafford he took 3 for 22 in the first innings and 6 for 37 in the second. He finished the series with 28 wickets at an average of 19.71.

After the Packer World Series, Roberts returned to Test cricket. In 1983 he was again near his best against the Indians in the Caribbean, taking 9 wickets in the first Test in Jamaica, and 8 in the fourth Test in Barbados, ending the series as the leading wicket-taker with 24 at an average of 22.70. He appeared in the last two Tests on the 1983-84 tour of India, and became the third West Indies bowler to take 200 wickets, achieving this goal in the final Test at Calcutta. He retired after the tour.

CAREER STATISTICS

Anderson Montgomery Everton Roberts • Antigua • 1951 • Right-arm fast bowler • Right-hand batsman
Test debut: v. England at Bridgetown, 1974

TESTS

Batting & Fielding	M	I	NO	Runs	HS	Ave	100	50	Ct	St
	47	62	11	762	68	14.94	0	3	9	0

Bowling	Balls	M	R	W	Ave	BBI	5	10	SR	Econ
	11135	382	5174	202	25.61	7-54	11	2	55.1	2.78

FIRST-CLASS (1969/70-1984)

Batting & Fielding	M	I	NO	Runs	HS	Ave	100	50	Ct	St
	228	291	67	3516	89	15.69	0	10	52	0

Bowling	Balls	M	R	W	Ave	BBI	5	10	SR	Econ
	-	-	18679	889	21.01	8-47	47	7	-	-

COURTNEY ANDREW WALSH

JAMAICA

Courtney Walsh was one of the most successful of fast bowlers, with a Test career spanning 17 years in which he bowled 5,004.1 overs and took 519 wickets.

He was also a consummate professional and dedicated sportsman whose performances became synonymous with the words 'courageous' and 'durable'. In the fifth Test against Australia in the 1996-97 series, Walsh tore his hamstring but continued to bowl for another 20 overs.

Although able to generate a great deal of pace, he was best known for his ability to maintain accurate line and length. This, coupled with skilful variation in pace, movement in the air and off the seam and the awkward bounce that his height (6' 5 1/2") afforded him, resulted in his taking the most ever Test wickets in a long and distinguished career.

Walsh took 519 wickets in 132 Tests at an average of 24.44. He also holds a Test batting record, which delicacy and decency forbids any mention of, other than to say that the total is 43.

Walsh and Curtly Ambrose were one of the finest fast bowling partnerships in the history of cricket. They took 421 wickets between them in 49 Tests. Walsh captained the West Indies for two years after Richardson stepped down. He was *Wisden* Cricketer of the Year in 1987.

Courtney Walsh retired in 2001. He is currently ambassador-at-large for Jamaica.

CAREER HIGHLIGHTS

Courtney Walsh made his first appearance for the West Indies on the 1984-85 tour of Australia, joining his illustrious team mates Holding, Marshall and Garner, as part of the famous four-pronged pace attack of the Lloyd era. But Walsh did not become a permanent fixture in the West Indies team until the 1986-87 tour of Pakistan, where he took 7 wickets in the second Test at Lahore.

Walsh had a brilliant tour of India in 1987-88. He took 5 for 54 in the first Test at Delhi; 5 for 54 and 4 for 40 in the second Test at Bombay; and 4 for 55 in the fourth Test at Madras, ending up with 26 wickets in the four Tests at an average of 16.80.

Walsh took the only hat trick of his career against Australia in 1988 in the first Test at Brisbane. He helped propel the West Indies to victory in the one-off Test against South Africa in 1992 with 4 for 31 off 22 overs in the second innings.

After making the West Indies team, up to 1993 Walsh was being used as the first change bowler. It was only after a long-term injury to Bishop that Walsh was used in 1994 as the new ball bowler with Ambrose against England in the Caribbean. So began one of the great fast bowling partnerships in the history of the game.

Taking over as captain of the West Indies team from Richardson against India in 1994, Walsh took 17 wickets at an average of 21.33, including 6 for 79 in the first Test at Bombay. In the two-Test series against New Zealand in 1995, Walsh, still as captain, took 7 for 37 and 6 for 18 in the second Test at Wellington as he led the West Indies to a 1-0 victory. These were also his best match figures.

In the series against Australia in the Caribbean in 1994-95, Walsh, with Richardson once again at the helm, was in fine form, taking 20 wickets at an average of 21.55, with best figures of 6 for 54 in the second Test in Antigua.

On the tour of England in 1995, Walsh took 26 wickets at an average of 30.23, with his best haul being 5 for 45 in the third Test at Edgbaston. He also claimed his 300th Test wicket during that series, in the sixth Test at The Oval. On the 1997 tour of Pakistan Walsh took his 350th Test wicket during the third Test at Karachi.

Walsh was replaced as captain by Brian Lara for the home series against England in 1998. He took 22 wickets at an average of 25.63 in the six Tests. In the last Test, in a blistering spell, Walsh picked up 4 wickets for 10 runs in 6.2 overs.

In the Caribbean against Australia in 1999, Walsh had a magnificent series. In the first Test in Trinidad he took 7 wickets, including his 400th wicket. He also took 7 wickets in the second Test in Jamaica, and 7 wickets in the third Test in Barbados, with figures of 5 for 39 in the second innings. He finished the series with 26 wickets.

On the 2000 tour of England Walsh was at his brilliant best, winning the Malcolm Marshall Trophy for leading wicket-taker (34) in a West Indies vs. England series, with figures of 5 for 36 and 3 for 22 in the first Test at Edgbaston; 4 for 43 and 6 for 74 in the second Test at Lord's; 4 for 50 and 1 for 19 in the third Test at Old Trafford; 4 for 51 in the fourth Test at Headingley; and 3 for 68 and 4 for 73 in the fifth Test at The Oval.

Against South Africa in 2001 Walsh took 6 for 61 in the second Test in Trinidad to become the first bowler ever to take 500 Test wickets.

Walsh played in his final Test, the fifth in Jamaica before his adoring fans. He took 6 for 93 in the match, and completed the series with 25 wickets at an average of 19.68. He then retired.

CAREER STATISTICS

Courtney Andrew Walsh • Jamaica • 1962 • Right-arm fast bowler • Right-hand batsman
Test debut: v. Australia at Perth, 1984

TESTS

Batting & Fielding	M	I	NO	Runs	HS	Ave	100	50	Ct	St
	132	185	61	936	30*	7.54	0	0	29	0

Bowling	O	M	R	W	Ave	BBI	5	10	SR	Econ
	5003.1	1144	12688	519	24.44	7-37	22	3	57.8	2.53

FIRST-CLASS (1981/82-2000/01)

Batting & Fielding	M	I	NO	Runs	HS	Ave	100	50	Ct	St
	429	558	158	4530	66	11.32	0	8	117	0

Bowling	O	M	R	W	Ave	BBI	5	10	SR	Econ
	14240	-	39233	1807	21.71	9-72	104	20	47.2	2.75

THE PRESEN

NT DAY

 **1995-PRESENT**

THIS IS THE PERIOD THAT HAS CREATED SO MUCH HEARTACHE FOR FANS OF WEST INDIES CRICKET. AFTER TWO DECADES OF WORLD SUPREMACY, IT IS HARD FOR FANS TO ACCEPT THAT THE WEST INDIES ARE STRUGGLING TO BEAT EVEN RELATIVELY WEAK TEAMS. BUT THERE IS ONE SHINING STAR IN THE FIRMAMENT OF WEST INDIES CRICKET: BRIAN LARA, THE ONLY GREAT PLAYER CHOSEN FROM THIS PERIOD. BUT THERE IS SO MUCH TALENT AROUND THAT WEST INDIES WILL SURELY RISE AGAIN, IN THE WORDS OF DAVID RUDDER, 'LIKE A RAGING FIRE'.

BRIAN CHARLES LARA

TRINIDAD

Brian Charles Lara is one of the most gifted batsmen in the history of cricket. He is in the line of greatness that produced Headley, the three 'W's, Sobers and Richards. Rated in the top ten of all time by most people, he is currently either number one or two in the world with Sachin Tendulkar of India. Lara, Tendulkar and Warne are the three most electrifying cricketers playing today.

Brian Lara is heir to the legendary Headley in more than one sense. Not only is he a genius but he has been fated to play cricket during the decline of the West Indies team since Richards retired in 1991, and has often had to carry the batting for the team with all the pressure that that entails.

The statistics certainly back up his reputation.
He previously held the highest Test score (375) and currently holds the highest first-class score (501). His current average of 50.45 ranks him among the greats.
No one since Bradman has accumulated scores as often and as fast as Lara.

Yet there is always a feeling that he has never quite fulfilled his promise.
He has gone through periods of poor form, inconsistency and apparent self-doubt.
His off-the-field behaviour has sometimes lacked maturity.
Nevertheless, by any standards he is a genius, even if a flawed one!

Lara has an unusually high backlift, a very good eye and feet like lightning. At the top of his form he is capable of dominating any bowling attack in the world from pace to spinners of the calibre of Warne or Muralitharan.
He has a full array of fine shots all round the wicket, but a glorious, effortless cover drive is probably his finest stroke.

Lara was *Wisden* Cricketer of the Year in 1995.

CAREER HIGHLIGHTS

Lara broke into the ranks of Test cricket on the West Indies tour of Pakistan in 1990-91. He scored 44 in his first Test innings.

Until the West Indies' 1992-93 tour to Australia, Lara was simply a batsman with great potential. That series, which West Indies won 2-1, made a star of the Trinidadian. He had made two half centuries in the first two matches, then struck his first Test century, 277 (including 38 fours), in the drawn third Test at Sydney, one of his greatest innings. He finished the tour with 466 runs at an average of 58.25.

If the series against Australia was Lara's spring, then the English tour of the Caribbean in 1993-94 was his glorious summer. Lara was in magnificent form, and keen to show the world that his Sydney innings was not a flash in the pan. He made 83 in the first Test, 167 (2 sixes and 25 fours) in the second, but saved the best for the last Test in Antigua. In a magnificent innings of intense concentration, Lara dominated the England attack. He hit 45 fours in surpassing Sir Garfield Sobers' 36-year-old record of 365, going on to make 375. He amassed 798 runs at an average of 99.75 for the series. The 'Prince' had arrived.

Lara then began playing for Warwickshire in the English County championship. He was an immediate success. He scored six centuries in his first seven innings: 147, 106, 120 not out, 136, 26, 140, and ended with an incredible 501 not out, the highest first-class score to date.

Returning to England with the West Indies in the summer of 1995, he was in fine form. He scored 145 in the fourth Test, 152 in the fifth Test, and 179 in the sixth Test, topping the batting with 765 runs at an average of 85.00.

Then Lara went through a bad patch with only the occasional good score. He was appointed captain of the West Indies in the series against England in 1998, which the West Indies won 3-1. Yet the captaincy only seemed to add to his troubles. Lara certainly hit bottom on the disastrous and humiliating tour of South Africa in 1998-99. He performed only moderately with the bat and led his team to a 5-0 drubbing in the Tests - the first whitewash for the West Indies - and 6-1 in the One-Day matches. There were calls for him to be sacked as captain. The future looked bleak, with a rampant Australia determined to dish out similar punishment to Lara's side in the series on the 1998-99 tour of the Caribbean. But Lara was to dig into his reserves and produce a magnificent effort. The West Indies managed only 51 in the first Test, the team's lowest total ever. But Lara's brilliance rescued the series. He hit 213 in the second Test in Jamaica, batting an entire day with Jimmy Adams as West Indies got back into and eventually won the match. Lara followed up with an unbeaten 153 as the West Indies won the third Test in Barbados by one wicket, rated by many as one of the greatest and most thrilling Test matches. Lara came to the crease at 78 for 3, and steered the West Indies to 311 for 9. These rank as two of his greatest innings to date. In the fourth and final Test, which was lost, he hit a first-innings 100 off 84 balls. Lara finished the series with 546 runs at an average of 91.09.

The following season, the West Indies' woeful away form continued. They lost all seven international matches in New Zealand, and 4-1 in Toronto in a One-Day series with India.

Following the New Zealand tour, Lara quit the captaincy. His form had fallen away dramatically and he had had a poor World Cup. After he said that he needed a break from cricket, many thought this would be the end of a special talent. But Lara's performance in the 2001 tour to Sri Lanka was staggering. Once again back at his best - apparently after a chat with Sir Garry Sobers - Lara dominated the Sri Lankan attack which was, in turn, dominating the rest of the West Indies batting order. In the three Tests he scored 178, 74, and 221, amassing 688 runs at an average of 114.66.

Back in the side for the tour by India, the much-hyped battle between Lara and Tendulkar failed to materialise. He made some typically flamboyant starts without capitalising.

Following solid performances in the 2002 World Cup, Lara was reappointed captain and had a good series against Australia in the Caribbean in 2003, scoring centuries in the first and second Tests. The captaincy seems to have brought about a new enthusiasm with the bat and in the field.

CAREER STATISTICS

Brian Charles Lara • Trinidad • 1969 • Left-hand batsman • Right-arm spin bowler
Test debut: v. Pakistan at Lahore, third Test, 1990-91

TESTS

Batting & Fielding	M	I	NO	Runs	HS	Ave	100	50	Ct	St
	92	161	4	7921	375	50.45	20	38	116	0

Bowling	O	M	R	W	Ave	BBI	5	10	SR	Econ
	10	1	28	0	-	-	0	0	-	2.80

FIRST-CLASS (1987/88-2002/03 LAST UPDATED 04/05/2003)

Batting & Fielding	M	I	NO	Runs	HS	Ave	100	50	Ct	St
	212	354	8	17328	501*	50.08	48	74	260	0

Bowling	O	M	R	W	Ave	BBI	5	10	SR	Econ
	84.4	5	411	4	102.75	1-1	0	0	127.0	4.85

APPENDIX I

COMPARATIVE STATISTICS FOR THE GREAT TWENTY-FIVE
~ BATTING & FIELDING ~

NAMES	TESTS	INNINGS	NO	HS	RUNS	AVE	100	50	CT
AMBROSE	98	145	29	53	1439	12.40	-	1	48
CHALLENOR	3	6	-	46	101	16.83	-	-	-
CONSTANTINE	18	33	-	90	635	19.24	-	4	28
DUJON	81	115	11	139	3322	31.94	5	16	267
GARNER	58	68	14	60	672	12.44	-	1	42
GIBBS	79	109	39	25	488	6.97	-	-	52
GREENIDGE	108	185	16	226	7558	44.72	19	34	96
HALL	48	66	14	50	818	15.73	-	2	11
HAYNES	116	202	25	184	7487	42.29	18	39	65
HEADLEY	22	40	4	270	2190	60.83	10	5	14
HOLDING	60	76	10	73	910	13.78	-	6	22
HUNTE	44	78	6	260	3245	45.06	8	13	16
KALLICHARRAN	66	109	10	187	4399	44.43	12	21	51
KANHAI	79	137	6	256	6227	47.53	15	28	50
LARA	92	161	4	375	7921	50.45	20	38	116
LLOYD	110	175	14	242*	7515	46.67	19	39	90
MARSHALL	81	107	11	92	1810	18.85	-	10	25
RAMADHIN	43	58	14	44	361	8.20	-	-	9
RICHARDS	121	182	12	291	8540	50.23	24	45	122
ROBERTS	47	62	11	68	762	14.94	-	3	9
SOBERS	93	160	21	365*	8032	57.78	26	30	109
WALCOTT	44	74	7	220	3798	56.68	15	14	53
WALSH	132	185	61	936	30*	7.54	-	-	29
WEEKES	48	81	5	207	4455	58.61	15	19	49
WORRELL	51	87	9	261	3860	49.48	9	22	43

APPENDIX II

COMPARATIVE STATISTICS FOR THE GREAT TWENTY-FIVE
~ BOWLING ~

NAMES	B	R	W	A	BB	5W	IOW
AMBROSE	22103	8501	405	20.99	8-45	22	3
CHALLENOR	-	-	-	-	-	-	-
CONSTANTINE	3583	1746	58	30.10	5-75	2	-
DUJON	-	-	-	-	-	-	-
GARNER	13169	5433	259	20.97	6-56	7	-
GIBBS	27115	8989	309	29.09	8-38	18	2
GREENIDGE	26	4	-	-	-	-	-
HALL	10421	5066	192	26.38	7-69	9	1
HAYNES	18	8	1	8.00	1-2	-	-
HEADLEY	398	230	-	-	-	-	-
HOLDING	12680	5898	249	23.68	8-92	13	2
HUNTE	270	110	2	55.00	1-17	-	-
KALLICHARRAN	406	158	4	39.50	2-16	-	-
KANHAI	183	85	-	-	-	-	-
LARA	60	28	-	-	-	-	-
LLOYD	1716	622	10	62.20	2-13	-	-
MARSHALL	17584	7876	376	20.94	7-22	22	4
RAMADHIN	13939	4579	158	28.98	7-49	10	1
RICHARDS	5170	1964	32	61.37	2-17	-	-
ROBERTS	11136	5174	202	25.61	7-54	11	2
SOBERS	21599	7999	235	34.03	6-73	6	-
WALCOTT	1194	408	11	37.09	3-50	-	-
WALSH	30019	12688	519	24.44	7-37	22	3
WEEKES	122	77	1	77.00	1-8	-	-
WORRELL	7141	2672	69	38.72	7-20	2	-